THE
PORT
VALE
MISCELLANY

THE
PORT VALE

MISCELLANY

PHIL SHERWIN

First published 2010

The History Press
The Mill, Brimscombe Port
Stroud, Gloucestershire, GL5 2QG
www.thehistorypress.co.uk

British Library Cataloguing in Publication Data.
A catalogue record for this book is available from the British Library.

ISBN 978 0 7524 5777 2

Typesetting and origination by The History Press
Printed in Great Britain

FOREWORD
by Robbie Earle MBE

I was honoured to be asked to write the foreword for this book on Port Vale, as there is no doubt that the club will always have a place in my heart. They are the club where I began my career and undoubtedly helped me to get to where I am today.

I was devastated when Stoke City released me as a youngster after I had broken my leg, but delighted to join Port Vale under the excellent tutelage of John Rudge, for whom I had the utmost respect, and still have. I always think players can be prouder when they play for their local club – which unfortunately happens less and less nowadays – but that was certainly true of myself every time I pulled on the black and white shirt of Port Vale.

I made my debut on the wing at Swindon Town in August 1982 when aged just 17, and I soon learned the tricks of the trade from experienced professionals such as Ernie Moss and Bob Newton. A few years later Ally Brown was my mentor when I played alongside him up front, although I later settled in midfield, usually alongside Ray Walker. There were some great days at the Vale, and beating Spurs 2–1 in the FA Cup in 1988 was definitely up there with the best.

Even that was topped though a year later, when we returned to the second tier of league football after a spell of 32 years by beating Bristol Rovers in the final of the play-offs. We played some great stuff that season and I was lucky enough to score the winning goal. I remember a photograph afterwards of me just sitting on the floor in the players' tunnel totally shattered and, I'm not ashamed to say, a bit tearful too. Being a local boy, I knew exactly what it meant to the fans to get up into the Second Division and restore local derbies against Stoke City, and I'm pleased to say that I played my part.

After nine years with the Vale it was still a wrench to leave, but at that point in my career I just had to take the opportunity of playing First Division football with Wimbledon, which became the Premier League a year later. Of course I will always follow the Vale's results and try to get to see them whenever I can.

This book details many anecdotes about what is really one of the smaller clubs in league football, but no less important, and many of the tales will both surprise and amuse you. I hope it is as an enjoyable read for you as it was for me.

INTRODUCTION

Writing this book about Port Vale has been a real labour of love, as they are my club, and have been for over 40 years. I evolved as the club statistician in the 1970s, when in the pre-internet days, details of Port Vale's past was not easy to come by. Even though we have never graced the very top level of English football, there are many stories to tell about a club that has been an important part of life in Stoke-on-Trent. Port Vale has been in existence for over 130 years, and among the many anecdotes are some quirky, some funny and some sad, and some never told in print before.

It's not a complete potted history of the club, but tries to cover all facets of its life and times throughout the years and all statistics are correct up to the end of the 2009/10 season. Hopefully it will be a good read and prompt many 'I never knew that' quotes as the information is digested.

Finally I would just like to thank Michelle Tilling and Richard Leatherdale from The History Press, Steve Askey for helping with the proof reading, Robbie Earle for the foreword, and as a point of reference, the *Sentinel* newspaper, as well as the many books on the club by Jeff Kent.

Let's hope that under Micky Adams we will soon have another promotion campaign to add to the text!

Phil Sherwin, 2010

IN THE BEGINNING

The actual details of the birth of Port Vale, the most romantically named club of them all, is shrouded in mystery with many different theories, but the following appears to be the most plausible.

In 1875 a group of men formed an athletics club with the main purpose of playing cricket; 'athletics' in those days not just meaning track and field. A year later they met again and decided to form a football club, a game that was becoming more and more popular. The meeting took place in an area known locally as Port Vale, although it wasn't an official place on the map. Nearby was Port Vale Wharf on the canal, Port Vale Brickworks, Port Vale Street, Port Vale Corn Mill and the actual meeting took place in Port Vale House.

When trying to come up with a name for the club, it is said that they just took the name of the house, but there was plenty of 'Port Vale' to choose from round and about. This area is about 2 miles from the club's present home in Burslem, Stoke-on-Trent. When they moved grounds to Burslem in 1884, they changed the club's name to Burslem Port Vale, dropping the prefix for the last time in 1909.

From humble beginnings they entered the FA Cup for the first time in 1885, became founder members of the Midland League in 1890, and were then founder members of the Football League Division Two in 1892.

WHAT'S IN A NAME?

What links Henry Cotton, Tommy Cooper, Dean Martin, John Surtees and Neville Chamberlain? No, not a celestial episode of *Come Dine With Me*, but all have played football for Port Vale. Or at least their namesakes have. All of them were locally born, Cotton in nearby Crewe and the other four in Stoke-on-Trent.

HE'S THE ONE

The club's most famous fan is singer Robbie Williams, who grew up a mere stone's throw from Vale Park. His parents ran a pub in the centre of Burslem called the Red Lion, before his father, Pete Conway, became the licensee at the Port Vale Social Club on the Hamil Road end of the ground in the mid-1970s. Robbie naturally became a fan and was a regular at games long before his musical career took over.

He often wears a Vale shirt at his concerts and in 2006 became the club's biggest shareholder by investing £249,000, the maximum allowed at the time with a limit being set at 24.9 per cent of the shares sold, which were then £1 million.

HEY, BIG SPENDER!

In October 1958 a new singing star was appearing locally in Hanley, and Vale manager Norman Low invited her along to watch the team play Oldham. Shirley Bassey was her name. That season Vale romped to the Fourth Division Championship scoring a club record 110 goals in the process, but this particular game ended 0–0! It was one of only four games the Vale failed to score in that season, but Ms Bassey couldn't have enjoyed it much because she hasn't been back since!

LIGHTEN UP

When the Vale hosted *Star Soccer*, ITV's Sunday afternoon highlights programme for a Fourth Division game against Sheffield United in October 1981 a problem occurred. It was a bit of a gloomy day and so the floodlights were switched on in the second half. Gary Newbon was in charge of the outside broadcast that day and while sitting in the directors' box with headphones on he suddenly began to go purple. He bellowed, 'The light's no good, the light's no good, we're losing the pictures! Someone turn the floodlights up a notch!'   .

Club secretary Richard Dennison dutifully scarpered out of the door and returned minutes later.

'Is that better, Gary?' he said.

'Yes, thanks, much better!' replied a relieved Mr Newbon.

Actually Richard hadn't done a thing, the lights were already as bright as they would go!

UNITED OVER THE VALE

What links England internationals David Beckham and Sir Bobby Charlton with Port Vale? Well, Beckham made his first senior start in a Manchester United shirt at Vale Park in a Coca-Cola Cup tie in September 1994. Vale Park was also the venue for Bobby Charlton's last ever Football League game, when he was the player-manager of Preston North End in March 1975.

HEAVY METAL HOLOCAUST

To raise much-needed funds the club staged a ten-hour music marathon in August 1981 called the Heavy Metal Holocaust. Bands appearing included Mahogany Rush, Triumph, Vardis, Riot and the headline act, Motörhead, who were fronted by locally-born Lemmy. Black Sabbath were due to appear, but pulled out late and were replaced by the Ozzy Osbourne Band, Ozzy having recently left Black Sabbath. Over 20,000 turned up and even many years later it was rated as one of the loudest amplifications ever at over 100,000 watts.

There was no trouble, and Vale made about £25,000, but after local residents had replaced their bouncing crockery and queued up to buy new eardrums, they have since made sure that it wouldn't happen again.

NICKNAMES

In the early years the Vale were briefly known as 'The Wanderers' because they moved home grounds so often, but that never really stuck. Because the other local team, Stoke City, were known as 'The Potters' after the area's main industry, a local newspaper reporter suggested that the Vale should be known as 'The Colliers' to reflect the large number of pits in the area, but again it never caught on.

When the club returned to the Football League in 1919 the club president, William Huntbach, had his eureka moment by decreeing that the club should be known as 'The Valiants' to reflect their struggle against adversity.

This one did stick, and they are known by that nickname to this very day.

ABANDONMENTS

The first recorded instance of Vale having a match abandoned occurred in February 1885. Over 5,000 spectators were present for a friendly against West Bromwich Albion and near the end of the game, with Vale losing 3–2, the ball burst. No one else had a ball, and so the game was abandoned!

On New Year's Day 1887, an FA Cup tie against Leek was abandoned because the pitch was deemed too dangerous.

Only three competitive games have ever been abandoned at Vale Park, with the first two occurring in its inaugural season. In December 1950, a monster of a snowstorm left vision impossible during a league game against Plymouth Argyle and the referee had had enough with the score at 0–0 after 56 minutes. A couple of months later, in February 1951, Vale were thrashing Crystal Palace 5–1 in a Third Division (South) game, having gone 3–0 ahead after only 10 minutes, but the referee called a halt to proceedings after an hour with everyone ankle-deep in mud. The player with the biggest gripe was striker Len Barber, who had scored four goals in the game! When it was replayed, two months later, the game ended 2–2.

The only other Vale Park abandonment occurred in November 1988. The home side were 3–1 ahead against Aldershot with just 13 minutes left when the fog became too thick to see properly. As it was Guy Fawkes' Night, there was some blame attached to local bonfires! At least when this one was replayed, Vale won 3–0.

There was a friendly abandonment in August 1996. A pre-season game against Wimbledon kicked off in a monsoon of biblical proportions and when a violent thunderstorm raged overhead the referee had understandably had enough after 33 minutes. The visitors were 1–0 ahead.

PLAYED FOR BOTH SIDES

One abandonment that is missing from the list on page 13 is arguably the most significant of them all. It was a Second Division game played at Charlton Athletic on Boxing Day 1932. Vale had played some great football and were 4–1 ahead after an hour when the fog thickened too much for the referee to carry on. In the Vale defence that afternoon was locally-born Jimmy Oakes making one of his 100-plus senior appearances for the Valiants. He would join Charlton a month later for £3,000.

When the abandoned game was replayed in the following April, Jimmy was in the Charlton line-up and therefore became the first, and possibly only, player to technically appear for both sides in the same game. Charlton won the replayed game 2–1 to rub salt into the wound. Jimmy went on to play over 200 games for the Addicks before settling back in his native Potteries where he died in 1992.

TIME FOR A DUCKING

In 1910 Port Vale were not in the Football League, and played in the North Staffs and District League. They just needed a draw to win the championship in the final game of the season, but it was away to their local rivals, Stoke reserves, who themselves could take the title with a victory.

To make sure of their chances, the Vale introduced four 'ringers', very good amateur footballers, including a goalkeeper by the name of Leigh Richmond Roose, also known as 'Dickie'. Dickie was a flamboyant, sometimes eccentric man, who had won 24 international caps for Wales and had played for Everton, Sunderland and, more importantly, Stoke previously.

This not surprisingly angered the Stoke supporters, and probably the Vale supporters as well when he played in a Stoke shirt under his goalkeeper's jersey during the game! The crowd of over 7,000 roared their disapproval as Vale went 2–0 ahead and Roose saved all that was thrown at him. During the second half a large section of the crowd invaded the pitch, surrounded Roose and started to push him towards the nearby River Trent. The Stoke forward, Vic Horrocks, later to rejoin the Vale, was knocked unconscious in the mêlée and Stoke chairman, the Revd Mr Hurst, appealed for calm.

Fortunately, order was restored before a ducking ensued but there was no alternative but to abandon the game. Roose claimed that he thought the game was a friendly and not a competitive fixture! The Staffs FA ordered the game to be replayed, but Vale refused and the championship was left unfilled, with Stoke having to close their ground for a fortnight.

Dickie went on to play for Huddersfield, Aston Villa and Arsenal and during the First World War he enlisted in the army, but was killed at the Battle of the Somme in 1916.

PENALTY KING

The most successful Port Vale penalty-taker was striker Andy Jones who managed 20 from a possible 23 attempts between January 1986 and September 1987. He took over the spot-kicking duties after Paul Maguire had missed a couple on the trot.

Not surprisingly he holds the record for scoring penalties in a season as well, scoring 12 in the 1986/87 campaign, when he also missed 3!

THE ONES WHO GOT AWAY

During the reign of Sir Stanley Matthews between 1965 and 1968, Port Vale put their future very much in the hands of a youth policy and had many trialists, particularly from the North-East and Scotland. Sir Stan told one young lad by the name of Ray Kennedy that he was to be released just after his sixteenth birthday in 1967 as he was 'too slow to be a footballer'.

Crestfallen, he returned to his native North-East and worked in a sweet factory but a year later he was signed by Arsenal, and during a career with the Gunners and later Liverpool, became one of the most decorated players in the game.

Another young North-Easterner had a short trial in the late 1960s. He went by the name of Brian Little, and he too was rejected before joining Aston Villa.

YOUNG BOYS OF BURSLEM

Football traditionally used to be played with five forwards in a team – two wingers, two inside forwards and a centre forward. Before the tactic disappeared in the early 1970s, Vale went down in history as fielding the youngest ever forward line for a game at Bradford City in January 1966.

Player-manager Jackie Mudie, along with general manager Sir Stanley Matthews, opted for youth and fielded Alex Donald (17), Paul Bannister (18), Roddy Georgeson (17), Mick Cullerton (17) and Paul Ogden (19). Four of them were making their debuts, with only Bannister ever having played in the first team before.

No other Football League team had ever fielded an all-teenage forward line before. The gamble didn't pay off though, as Vale lost 2–0.

BLANK CHEQUE

When Third Division Port Vale defeated then First Division Cardiff City 2–0 on their own ground in the fourth round of the FA Cup in January 1954, the Welshmen were very impressed by Vale winger Colin Askey – so much so that they offered £25,000 for his services, a very good fee considering the British record at the time was £34,500. Vale turned this down, and then Cardiff made the extraordinary gesture of offering a blank cheque instead!

Vale still said no, impressive to the supporters but not so much for the bank manager. Colin himself was quite happy to stay at the Vale, and it should also be noted that because of the maximum wage at the time, footballers did not benefit by moving clubs. In those days a footballer was no better off salary-wise playing for Manchester United than he was for Darlington.

HE'S THE GAFFER

The full list of the men in the Port Vale hot seat is as follows:

Sam Bennion	1896–1905
Tom Clare	1905–6
Sam Bennion	1906–7
Arthur Walker	1911–13
Harry Myatt	1913–14
Tom Holford	1914–17
Jack Cameron	1918–19
Joe Schofield	1919–29
Tom Morgan	1929–32

Tom Holford	1932–6
Warney Cresswell	1936–7
Tom Morgan	1937–9
Billy Frith	1944–6
Gordon Hodgson	1946–51
Ivor Powell	1951
Freddie Steele	1951–7
Norman Low	1957–62
Freddie Steele	1962–5
Jackie Mudie	1965–7
Sir Stanley Matthews	1967–8
Gordon Lee	1968–74
Roy Sproson	1974–7
Colin Harper	1977
Bobby Smith	1977–8
Denis Butler	1978–9
Alan Bloor	1979
John McGrath	1979–83
John Rudge	1983–99
Brian Horton	1999–2004
Martin Foyle	2004–7
Dean Glover	2007
Lee Sinnott	2007–8
Dean Glover	2008–9
Micky Adams	2009–

NB: between 1907 and 1911 the club was run by a committee, so there was no manager as such.

JUST NOT CRICKET

Only one Test cricketer has played for the Port Vale first team, Harry Howell, who was the club's leading scorer in the 1918/19 season when the club played in the Lancashire Regional League. He also played for Wolves and Stoke before his cricketing career with Warwickshire took over in the early 1920s and he went on to be picked for five Test matches. A right-arm fast bowler, he once took all 10 wickets in an innings against Yorkshire, but declining health shortened his career. He died in 1932, aged just 41.

Ken Higgs and Bob Taylor, who made many Test appearances between them, were on the Vale's books as apprentices in the early 1960s, but never graduated to the first team.

Gordon Hodgson, the Vale manager between 1946 and 1951, had previously played 56 games for Lancashire County Cricket Club before the Second World War, as well as playing football for Liverpool and England.

Ian Buxton was a striker who played for 14 years with Derbyshire County Cricket Club and played football in the winter with Derby County, Luton Town, Notts County and Port Vale, who he joined on a 3-month deal in December 1969. He did well with 6 goals in 18 appearances, helping the club to secure promotion from Division Four, but left before the end of the campaign to return to cricket. He captained Derbyshire for the next three seasons, retiring in 1973.

Vale player Arthur Jepson was a medium-pace bowler for Nottinghamshire in county cricket but he also became the club's goalkeeper in 1938 making over 50 senior appearances for them. He later played for Stoke City and Lincoln City, but continued his cricketing prowess to take over 1,000 wickets in his career. Later he became a first-class cricket umpire, graduating to international level.

Fred Gardner played four times for the Vale in the war leagues in 1946 before turning his attention to cricket, playing 14 years as an opening batsman for Warwickshire. He then had a further 3 years as a first-class umpire.

REFEREE!

In the early days of their Football League career, Port Vale had an inside forward by the name of James Mason, who scored 9 goals in 51 appearances between 1892 and 1897. He was a cocky individual and often used to try to hit the clock on the local church tower while supposedly training.

The club gave him a *sine die* suspension for offensive conduct in February 1897 and freed him a year later. With his career in tatters, what did he do? He became a referee, that's what! Quite a top one as well. He refereed four England international matches, including one at Hampden Park against Scotland, and the 1909 FA Cup final, won by Manchester United. That's the way to do it.

FAMOUS SONS

Harry McShane, who played 3 games for Port Vale during the 1945 war leagues, was little known at the Vale, but his son Ian went on to be a successful actor. He has made many films but is probably best remembered for the TV series, *Lovejoy*. Harry played league football for Blackburn Rovers, Huddersfield Town, Bolton Wanderers, Manchester United, Oldham Athletic and later became a scout for Manchester United, Wes Brown being one of his discoveries.

Terry Owen made 20 appearances for the Vale during the 1979/80 season. He also became a father during that time, and son Michael (whom you may have heard of) has played for Liverpool, Manchester United, Real Madrid and England among others.

Robert Carter made 89 appearances for the Vale between 1905 and 1907 but his son Raich went on to have a more illustrious career. He played for Sunderland, Derby County, Hull City and England, besides managing Hull City, Leeds United, Mansfield and Middlesbrough.

On the other side of the coin, Ian Brightwell, who played for the Vale between 2002 and 2004, had a couple of famous parents. His mother is Ann Packer, who won a gold medal for Great Britain in the 800 metres in the 1964 Olympics in Tokyo, while father Robbie Brightwell won a silver at the 1964 Olympics in the 4 x 400 metres relay, and a gold at the 1962 European championships.

RECORD SALE

Port Vale's record transfer fee received is £2 million from Wimbledon for Gareth Ainsworth in October 1998. He had only been with the Vale for 13 months, scoring 11 goals in 59 senior appearances, but his all-action style in what is now called the Championship soon earned him a move to the Premier League.

He was signed for £500,000, another club record, along with that of Dave Brammer, from Lincoln City in September 1997. He went on to play for Preston North End, Walsall, Cardiff City, QPR (where he had a spell as manager) and Wycombe Wanderers.

QUICKEST GOALS

Midfielder Ian Bogie holds the distinction of scoring the fastest ever goal for the Vale, notching after just 12 seconds against local rivals Stoke City in a First Division game in March 1996. It was the only goal of the game.

Michael Husbands scored after 14 seconds against Nottingham Forest in September 2006. The game ended 1–1 but Michael was sent off in the second half.

Striker John Froggatt marked his Vale debut with a goal after 15 seconds in a 4–0 victory over Exeter City in February 1978.

The fastest own goal scored in the Vale's favour was scored by Lincoln City's Ian Pearce in February 2010, when he turned a back pass into his own net after just 21 seconds. Vale went on to win 4–0.

MISSED TRAIN

When Port Vale began their days in the Football League back in September 1892, their first game was away to Small Heath, nowadays called Birmingham City. Preparations were in hand, but on the day of the game, striker Billy Beats missed the train and the side were forced to play with 10 men! Not surprisingly they lost 5–1. Beats still finished the season as the club's top scorer, though – a feat he repeated on another two occasions, and he also went to play for England after a move to Wolverhampton Wanderers.

Trains were not to be relied upon in those days, as in February 1895 both full-backs read the timetable wrong for a trip to Notts County. They tried to catch a train that only ran on market days, missed the game and with another player simply not turning up, Vale played most of the game with just 8 men! They lost 10–0, equalling a club record.

UNBEATEN RUNS

The longest the Vale have ever gone without defeat is 19 games, both in the league and in all competitions.

After winning their final game of the 1968/69 season at Bradford Park Avenue, Vale went undefeated for the first 18 league games of the following season, making 19 altogether. Altogether it featured 11 wins and 8 draws as manager Gordon Lee put together a promotion-winning team in the Fourth Division. It came to an end though at Scunthorpe United in November 1969 when the home team, featuring a youthful Kevin Keegan in their side, won 2–1. What was galling for the Vale was that the Scunthorpe goals were an own goal and a penalty.

HOME COMFORTS

Port Vale were unbeaten in league games at home between October 1952 and October 1954 – a total of 42 games. The game which preceded that run, in October 1952, was a 1–0 defeat by Accrington Stanley, and that was the club's only home defeat in a run of 72 games lasting over 3 years.

FOOTBALL LEAGUE RECORDS

Vale are the owners of three all-time Football League records, two proud and one not so proud.

Most clean sheets in a season   30 (achieved in 1953/54)

Scoring 4 or more in consecutive league games   7 times (April–September 1893)

The full scoring list is as follows:

8 April 1893	Northwich Victoria	(A)	4–2
2 September 1893	Ardwick	(H)	4–2
9 September 1893	Walsall T.S.	(A)	5–0
16 September 1893	Crewe Alexandra	(H)	4–2
18 September 1893	Middlesbrough Ironopolis	(H)	4–0
23 September 1893	Northwich Victoria	(A)	5–1
30 September 1893	Small Heath	(H)	5–0

The not-so-proud record is the 10–0 home defeat by Sheffield United in December 1892, which is the only time a Football League team has conceded 10 in a home game.

A FAMILY AFFAIR

The name Sproson will always be linked to Port Vale, as three members of that family have amassed almost 1,400 senior appearances between them, almost certainly a unique record. Roy Sproson is the most well known after a playing career that lasted from 1950 to 1972 when he made 836 appearances, a one-club record only beaten by John Trollope of Swindon Town. (In league games only, he is third behind Trollope and Jimmy Dickinson of Portsmouth.) When he finished playing, Roy became youth coach and then the first-team manager for 3 years, between 1974 and 1977. It all ended on a sour note though when results dictated that Roy was sacked in October 1977. He refused an offer of returning to the post of youth coach, unscrewed his name plate from the door of the manager's office and vowed never to return to Vale Park ever again. Sadly he never did and died aged 66 in 1997.

Roy's brother Jess played 38 wartime games for the club and nephew Phil lies second on the club's all time appearance records with exactly 500 senior appearances. Phil was a solid centre-half between 1977 and 1989 before moving on to Birmingham City for £50,000. The legend lives on, with Sproson Park behind the Bycars end of the ground and Roy Sproson Way, the main thoroughfare from the main road to the entrance of the football club.

A statue of Roy is due to be sited outside the main entrance and unveiled sometime in 2010.

THEY DIED WITH THEIR BOOTS ON

Before the advent of league football, Burslem Port Vale signed a Scottish striker by the name of Frank McGinnis in 1889. He started to bang the goals in left, right and centre, and was the club's leading scorer for three successive seasons in the Midland League. First Division Stoke tried to entice him away, offering a transfer fee of £30 and £50 up front to the player with a guinea a game thereafter, but the approach was rebuffed.

Frank was mentioned in newspapers as having been the 'best centre forward ever to leave Scotland' and when Vale were elected to the newly formed Second Division of the Football League, hopes were high of an immediate promotion.

Just 6 weeks before the season though, Frank suffered a serious kidney disease and died aged just 23. Who knows what would have happened if Frank had lived up to his reputation?

Thomas Butler was a forward who joined the Vale in 1922. He was top scorer in the 1922/23 season, but then in November 1923, after scoring in a 1–1 draw at Clapton Orient, Tommy suffered a compound fracture of the arm. Septic poisoning set in and he sadly died of lockjaw 8 days later in Hackney Hospital.

GYPSY JOE

In 1891 Vale signed a new goalkeeper called Martin Joseph Frail, known as Joe. He was a traditional gypsy, lived in a caravan throughout his career and always wore a knotted handkerchief around his neck whenever he played.

He played in the Vale's first ever league game and had made 30 appearances when he failed to catch the train to Rotherham Town for a league game in 1893. Not surprisingly club officials asked him for an explanation but Joe refused to give one! They suspended him until he did so, but he never did and remained on the sidelines for the rest of the season.

Vale were then forced to release him and he later played for Glossop North End, Derby County and Middlesbrough. He had two spells at Boro, both ending after court appearances for misdemeanours. After his football career, he continued his Romany lifestyle.

SHORTEST CAREER

Two players share the distinction of the shortest ever first team career with Port Vale – both lasted just 1 minute!

Darrell Clarke joined Vale on loan from Hartlepool for a month in September 2005. He was only signed as cover, but actually only got onto the field for the last minute of a 3–2 victory over Walsall, replacing Chris Cornes.

Luke Chapman came through the ranks at the Vale and came on as a substitute for Danny Glover in the last minute of the final game of the 2007/08 season at Southend United. He almost scored with his first touch as a ball flew across the Southend box. He was only 17 at the time, and became a professional the following season, but injury limited his options and he was released in 2009.

FATHER AND SON

The only father and son partnership to score senior goals for the Vale are the Glovers, Dean and Danny. Dean scored 20 goals as a central defender between 1989 and 1998 while his son Danny managed 4 during his time as a striker between 2007 and 2010.

The only other father and son combination to play league football for the club are Peter and Robert Purcell, who were both full-backs and never scored a goal between them! Peter made 166 appearances between 1919 and 1924 and son Robert made 96 between 1939 and 1949.

MAN OF THE CLOTH

Port Vale half-back Norman Hallam was a regular member of the team between 1946 and 1948. He quit the game in July 1948 when he was accepted as a Methodist minister. One sad task that came his way was to conduct the funeral service for Vale manager Gordon Hodgson, who died in office in 1951. He resumed his football career in 1952, but travelling from his Birmingham home restricted his appearances and he left the Vale a year later.

DEBUT AT 11

Which professional footballer made his first team bow with the Vale when aged just 11? The answer is striker Danny Glover, who came on as a substitute in a testimonial match for Martin Foyle in 2001. Danny's father Dean also played in the game and because Martin was his best mate they allowed their children to come on as substitutes. Martin's son Lee actually scored a penalty! Robbie Williams and Jonathan Wilkes also played in the game.

TOP TEN GATES

The top ten highest attendances the Vale have ever appeared in front of are as follows:

68,221   v West Brom (FA Cup semi-final), March 1954
53,471   v West Brom (play-off final), May 1993
52,327   v Liverpool (A) (FA Cup 4th round), January 1964
50,684   v Tottenham Hotspur (A) (FA Cup 4th round), January 1955
49,768   v Aston Villa (H) (FA Cup 5th round), February 1960
49,692   v Burnley (A) (FA Cup 4th round), January 1950
49,500   v Stoke City (A) (FA Cup 3rd Round), January 1951
49,468   v Sunderland (A) (FA Cup 4th Round), January 1962
46,872   v Aston Villa (A) (FA Cup 5th Round), February 1977
46,777   v Stoke City (A) (Division 2), September 1954

Unfortunately the Vale didn't win any of the matches listed above! The largest attendance which they have won in front of is the 42,000 who witnessed the 2–0 FA Cup victory over Blackpool in February 1954.

HOME COMFORTS

The top ten highest attendances for a Port Vale home game are as follows:

49,768 v Aston Villa (FA Cup 5th round), February 1960
44,278 v Everton (FA Cup 4th round), January 1956
42,179 v Liverpool (FA Cup 4th round), January 1964
42,000 v Blackpool (FA Cup 5th round), February 1954
41,674 v Stoke City (Division Two), April 1955
37,261 v Stoke City (Division Two), October 1955
30,196 v Newport County (Division Three South), August
        1950
29,415 v Fulham (Division Two), December 1954
28,206 v Sunderland (FA Cup 4th round), January 1962
26,941 v Southport (Division Three North), April 1954

NB: the above does not include the 40,977 who watched the FA Cup third-round replay with Stoke City in January 1951, which was technically a 'home' game, but was played at Stoke City as Vale Park was unfit.

BOGEY TEAMS

In football there are always some teams that certain sides just can't beat, for no real reason despite whatever the clubs' respective fortunes. Port Vale's biggest bogey has undoubtedly been Walsall. Between April 1965 and September 1986, the teams met 26 times home and away, without the Vale recording a single victory; 20 of those games were in the league and 6 in the cups.

Although the run has been broken at home, it still stands for away games in the league, and the Vale are without a victory there in 26 visits, dating back to when Queen Elizabeth II was on her honeymoon in November 1947. They have had two cup victories there though, an FA Cup third-round success in 1956 and a Littlewoods Cup victory in 1989, the Vale's last ever visit to Fellows Park.

On the other side of the coin, the team that Vale have been the biggest bogey to is near-neighbours Crewe Alexandra. From April 1968 until January 1998 the two clubs met on 19 occasions without the Vale losing at all, and strangely the two Crewe victories either side of that barren spell both occurred at Vale Park. Vale have a decent record at the Alexandra Stadium though, losing just 2 of their last 17 visits in all competitions.

Crewe have suddenly become a bogey side at Vale Park though, winning 6 of their last 7 visits in four different competitions between 2002 and 2010.

WEMBERLEE!

For many years Port Vale fans never thought that they would ever see their team walk out at Wembley stadium, but then just like buses, two came along at once. In May 1993 Vale reached the final of the Autoglass Trophy, the cup competition for lower league clubs. They outplayed Stockport County to win it as well, 2–1, but just 8 days later they were back in the shadow of the twin towers for the Third Division play-off final against West Brom. A lot of fans could not afford to travel to both games within a short space of time and so the 25,000 following for the first game lessened to around 10,000 for the second one, even though it was more important.

It turned out to be a game too far for the team as well, as West Brom triumphed 3–0. After that season, the powers that be scheduled the Autoglass Trophy final and all its future guises to be played earlier in the season to prevent a team reaching both that and the play-off final being unfairly penalised.

The Vale did reach Wembley again, in the last Anglo-Italian Cup final in 1996 when they lost 5–2 against Genoa.

FOREIGN LEGION

Port Vale have been represented by players from 26 different countries altogether. Aside from the numerous ones from England, Scotland, Wales, Northern Ireland and the Republic of Ireland, they are:

France – Stephane Pounewatchy, Christophe Horlaville
Sweden – Jan Jansson, Tobias Mikaelsson
Austria – Andreas Lipa
Australia – Chris Herd
New Zealand – Chris Killen, Dave Mulligan
Holland – Robin Van Der Laan, Mark Snijders, Arjan van Heusden, Rogier Koordes, Tyrone Loran, Jermaine Holwyn, Nico Jalink
Pakistan – Adnam Ahmed
Canada – Randy Samuel
Nigeria – Reuben Agboola, George Abbey, Dolapo Olaoye, Akpo Sodje
Trinidad & Tobago – Chris Birchall, Tony Rougier, Hector Sam
Finland – Ville Viljanen
St Kitts – Sagi Burton, Callum Willock
South Africa – Paul Byrne, Justin Miller, Ken Fish
Jamaica – Robbie Earle, Onandi Lowe, Bob Hazell (became a British citizen)
Sierra Leone – Malvin Kamara
Norway – Robin Berntsen
Cameroon – Simon Pierre Mvondo (known as Atangana)
Lithuania – Louis Bookman (became an Irish citizen)
India – George Price (became a British citizen)
Egypt – Roddy Georgeson (became a British citizen)
Faroe Islands – Claus Jorgensen

THE LONG AND THE SHORT OF IT

The honour of the player with the longest name to play for Port Vale goes to Sagi Burton, who scored 4 goals in 99 appearances between 2000 and 2002. Sagi is what he is known as, but his real moniker is a stonking 32 letters – Osagyefo Lenin Ernesto Burton-Godwin. A mention in despatches must go those who run him close:

Louis James Arthur Oscar Buckhalter (31) (known as Louis Bookman)
William Martin Melville Henderson (30)
Reuben Omojola Folasanje Agboola (29)
Darren Richard Lorenzo Beckford (28)
Jermaine Titano Benito Holwyn (26)
Idoro Akpoeyere Ujoma Sodje (24) (known as Akpo)

On the other side of the coin, the players with the shortest full names contain just 8 letters, being Ian Bogie and Gary West.

SEVENTH HEAVEN

When Port Vale thrashed Chesterfield 7–1 in a Third Division game back in September 1960, little did they know that almost 50 years later they would still be waiting to notch another 7. True, scores like that are a rare occurrence in league football, but no other Football League club has gone so long without passing six in a senior game.

For the record, the scorers in that Third Division game were Ted Calland (2), Brian Jackson, Stan Steele, Cliff Portwood, Terry Miles and Denis Fidler, while those that could say 'I was there' numbered 10,104.

WELSH CUP

Just to add credence to those who think that Port Vale is somewhere between Port Talbot and Ebbw Vale, the club did actually enter the Welsh Cup in the 1933/34 season. Right up until 1995, Football League clubs in a reasonable proximity to Wales were allowed to enter. At the time the Vale were well placed in the Second Division with a chance of promotion, so to avoid the possibility of injury, fielded a complete reserve side in the Welsh Cup – so squad rotation was alive and kicking before Messrs Ferguson and Wenger were even born!

League sides didn't come into the competition until the sixth round (last 16) and Vale made their bow with a 1–1 draw at Rhyl. They won the replay 2–0.

In the quarter-finals they again drew away from home, 3–3 at Bristol Rovers, before winning the replay at the Old Recreation Ground 2–1. The semi-finals were played on neutral grounds, and Vale faced Bristol City at Chester. Vale's hopes of silverware were undone by the eventual winners of the trophy, Bristol City, going down 1–0.

DEBENHAMS CUP

This was a little known competition for the two teams from outside the top two divisions who progressed the furthest in the FA Cup. It only lasted for two seasons, but Port Vale were in the first final in the 1976/77 season having reached the fifth round of the FA Cup, losing 3–0 at Aston Villa. The team's opposition were Chester City and the final was played over two legs with the first leg taking place at Vale Park on 16 May 1977. A crowd of 3,459 turned up to see Vale put one hand on the trophy with a 2–0 victory, courtesy of goals by Neil Griffiths and Ken Beamish.

Eight days later in the second leg at Sealand Road, though, Chester had other ideas and soon went 2–0 ahead. Beamish pulled a goal back, meaning that Chester then had to score 4 to win, but they went and did so, taking the trophy 4–3 on aggregate. After the following season, the competition was then scrapped.

YOUNG GUNS

The youngest player to represent the Vale in a first-team game was Malcolm Mackenzie, who was just 15 years and 347 days old when he made his debut on the left wing against Newport County on 12 April 1966. Vale won 3–0 and Malcolm turned professional at the end of the following season, but he made just a further 7 appearances for the first team before being released in 1968. The top ten youngest players to have made their Vale debuts are as follows:

Malcolm Mackenzie   15 yrs 347 days
v Newport County April 1966

Stuart Chapman   15 yrs 362 days
v Lincoln City May 1967

Ronnie Allen   16 yrs 77 days
v Wrexham (War league) April 1945

Malcolm Gibbon   16 yrs 201 days
v Brentford May 1967

Mark Chamberlain   16 yrs 273 days
v Scunthorpe United August 1978

Billy Paynter   16 yrs 294 days
v Walsall May 2001

James Lawrie   16 yrs 327 days
v Morecambe (FA Cup) November 2007

Clinton Boulton   16 yrs 354 days
v Hull City December 1964

William Tunnicliffe	17 yrs 32 days
	v Charlton Athletic February 1937
Kenny Beech	17 yrs 41 days
	v Brighton April 1975

NB: the youngest FA Cup debutant is Ronnie Allen, who was 16 yrs and 306 days old when he played against Wellington Town in November 1945.

The youngest first team goalscorer was Ronnie Allen when he scored against Norwich City in a wartime Football League game in August 1945 aged just 16 years 228 days. In a proper Football League game, the title falls to Mark Chamberlain who scored in a 3–2 defeat at Huddersfield Town in April 1979 when aged just 17 years 150 days.

DIVISION THREE CUP

The Third Division's North and South sections both held a cup competition purely for teams in their respective divisions between 1934 and 1939. Vale were relegated from the Second Division in 1936 and became eligible for the Northern version in 1936/37. They defeated Mansfield (2–0), Stockport County (4–0) and Rotherham United (1–0), which put them into the semi-finals. It was here that the run came to an end, losing 3–0 at the now-defunct Chester. The following season they had another go, but lost in the first round 2–0 at Tranmere Rovers after a 1–1 draw.

Due to being geographically in the Midlands, the team often moved between the North and the South in Division Three depending on who was relegated and competed in the southern version of the divisional cup in 1938/39. Walsall (4–0), Mansfield, who had also changed divisions (3–1), and

Ipswich (2–0), were all defeated on the way to another semi-final appearance. This took place at QPR and ended 0–0. Crowds for this competition were very low, usually less than 1,000, so teams often lost money, particularly when travelling a long distance. QPR weren't too thrilled about the prospect of travelling to the Vale for a replay, and with the winners facing a two-legged final against Torquay United, both clubs asked the Football League to scrap the competition! At first they refused, but agreed after a bit of pressure. The Second World War then halted league football for seven years, and these divisional cups never saw the light of day again.

THE STEELE CURTAIN

When Freddie Steele became the Vale manager in December 1951 he effectively transferred himself, because he was the player-manager at Mansfield Town, and took over the same role at Vale Park! He retired from playing a year later but developed a defensive system of play unique for its day, but based on the Arsenal team of the 1930s. Vale finished runners-up in the Third Division (North) in the 1952/53 season, but in those days only one team was promoted so they set about putting that right the following season.

They did it in style, as they took over at the top of the table after just 4 games and remained there for the rest of the campaign. Their defensive record was remarkable, as when Chesterfield visited Vale Park in February 1954, they had only conceded 1 goal at home! Chesterfield actually scored twice, an event of seismic proportions, but the total of 5 conceded at home by the season's end is still a Football League record for a 46-game season.

The overall total of goals conceded of 21 was a record for many years, only being beaten by Gillingham's total of 20 conceded in the 1995/96 season. Vale still have the honour of the most clean sheets though – 30 – 29 of which were kept by Ray King, an England 'B' international goalkeeper. The team were unbeaten at home, the only season they have ever achieved that feat, and they only lost 3 away games, ironically all in the far north of the country! Those defeats came at Gateshead, Workington and Hartlepool. That was the season the team almost reached Wembley as well, losing in the semi-finals of the FA Cup to West Brom after leading at half time.

SIR STANLEY MATTHEWS

Port Vale never normally get a mention in Stanley Matthews stories, but being born in Hanley, he actually grew up as a Vale fan, as that is where the club played their home games in those days. Another twist is that after he began his career with rivals Stoke City, he scored the first senior goal of his career against the Vale at their Old Recreation Ground, a matter of yards from where he was born.

He was a member of the famous Blackpool team knocked out of the FA Cup by the Vale in 1954, but his next link with the club was when he became general manager in 1965. It generated much publicity, and the team played numerous friendlies as it seemed everybody wanted to see such a famous footballing icon.

Stan and team manager Jackie Mudie put their faith in youth, fielding many youngsters, including an all-teenage front five, which had never been done before. When Mudie resigned in 1967, Stan took over the reins completely, but the 1967/68 season was not a memorable one. The club were found guilty of making illegal payments to players and forced to seek re-election to the league. They duly were re-elected and although Stan reverted to general manager with Gordon Lee resuming team affairs, he slowly drifted out of the picture and left.

TREBLE HAT-TRICK

When Port Vale played Aldershot in a run-of-the-mill Third Division (South) game in September 1947, little did they realise it would make history. In the event, Vale won 6–4, unusual in itself, but what made it stand out even more was that three hat-tricks were scored in the game. Maurice Jones and Ronnie Allen scored threesomes for the Vale, with Alex McNicholl doing likewise for the Shots. Ironically the man who scored the other Aldershot goal from the penalty spot, Ted Smith, was born in Stoke-on-Trent.

GOLDEN GOAL

To spice the game up a bit, the powers that be decided to use a golden goal as a way of deciding the victors in the Football League Trophy from 1994 onwards. It means that if a game went to extra time, the scorers of the first goal win the game and it ends immediately.

It was called the LDV Vans Trophy when the rule involved the Vale on two occasions. The first time it happened was in March 2001 for a Northern semi-final tie against local rivals Stoke City. The game had been switched to Stoke's Britannia Stadium when Vale Park was unfit and the game stood at 1–1 after 90 minutes. A hand ball gave Vale a penalty on the stroke of half time in extra time though, and Marc Bridge-Wilkinson gleefully smashed it home to end the game.

The other occasion was a third-round tie in December 2002 at Shrewsbury Town, five days after the Vale had gone into administration. That also went to extra time at 1–1, but Shrewsbury got the winner in the 110th minute. The rule was scrapped in 2004.

GROUND SWAP

When the Vale opened their new ground at Vale Park in 1950, they had a few problems with their drains. The pitch was built on an old marl hole and had a clay base, so water would not drain properly, and any rain just turned the surface into a mudbath. As winter set in, the pitch was just unplayable and had frozen over in December. For the home game on Christmas Day against Bristol Rovers, they hit on the idea of playing it at Stoke City, which was only 5 miles away. It all worked out okay, and 13,250 turned up for the game, which kicked off at 11 a.m., but it ended in a disappointing goalless draw.

As it happens, that season the Vale were drawn away to Stoke in the third round of the FA Cup a couple of weeks later. It ended in a 2–2 draw and with Vale Park still being unfit, the replay also took place at the Victoria Ground. Vale lost 1–0 to a goal 4 minutes from time, but the crowd of 40,977 was at the time the largest 'home' attendance the club had ever had.

The favour for the ground loan was reversed in January 1976, when the Vale directors offered Stoke the use of their facilities after one of the stands at the Victoria Ground had been damaged by strong winds. The offer was taken up and over 20,000 turned up to see Stoke beat Middlesbrough 1–0. It is so far the only time that Vale Park has staged top-flight football, and the historic goalscorer was the late Ian Moores, who played a couple of friendly games for the Vale towards the end of his career.

Another ground swap occurred unusually in the Northern semi-finals of the LDV Vans Trophy in March 2001. Vale had been drawn at home to Stoke, but were having problems with their pitch at the time. First it was postponed through frost, then it was waterlogged a fortnight later, and with the pitch still unfit a week after that, the Football League insisted on switching the game to the Britannia Stadium. Vale took the lead through Micky Cummins only for Nicky Mohan to send the game into extra time 3 minutes from the end. In those days ties were decided by the golden goal rule, whereby the first goal in extra time wins it. When Vale were awarded a penalty in the 105th minute, Marc Bridge-Wilkinson scored it, and that was the end of the game as 3,000 Vale fans ecstatically partied in the away end!

FA CUP PULL-OUT

The Vale entered the FA Cup for the first time in the 1885/86 season and it proved to be a rather bizarre experience. They progressed from the second round to the fifth without really winning a game and then pulled out with a place in the quarter-finals at stake!

It all began rather modestly, with a first-round victory at Chirk (3–0) and a second-round win over the Welsh Druids, 5–1 after a replay. Then the fun started. In the third round Vale were drawn away to Leek, and were 3–2 ahead in extra time (in a game in which there was no love lost between the two teams), when a pitch invasion caused the game to be abandoned. Leek protested that the game was being played in darkness because of Vale's late arrival and their appeal was upheld and a replay was ordered. Leek really wanted to be awarded a victory, and then pulled out rather than face a replay!

In the fourth round Vale were awarded a bye, one of fourteen with only two ties actually being played, and then faced a home tie against Brentwood, a southern university team, in the fifth round with a tie against the cup-holders Blackburn Rovers awaiting the winners.

Over 6,000 fans saw Vale win 2–1 on a swamp of a pitch at Moorland Road, but afterwards Brentwood complained that the pitch was unfit. Bizarrely Blackburn supported their appeal, also having played recently on the Vale ground in a friendly. The FA ordered a replay but as the Vale ground was obviously deemed not suitable, it took place at the County Ground in Derby.

Vale were roared on by 2,000 of their fans and came back from 4–2 down to draw 4–4 with two late goals. This meant a trip to Brentwood, but as they were a university team, their ground was not enclosed and so there would be no gate receipts. Vale were already feeling hard done by, having two victories in the run ruled out by the FA, and faced with an expensive trip to London, pulled out of the competition. Blackburn Rovers went on to win the trophy for the third time in succession, the last time such a feat happened, and who knows if they would have achieved it had they had to play the Vale?

GREAT ESCAPE (1)

Vale were in the Second Division in the 1931/32 season and with just two games to go they looked doomed to relegation. There were only 2 points for a win in those days and the Vale were 3 points from safety, with a worse goal average than the only team that they could realistically catch, Barnsley. Form didn't offer any hope either, as only 3 points had been taken from the previous twelve games, the last six of which had all been lost. Not surprisingly only 4,663 spectators turned up for their final home game of the season, less than half of that season's average.

In the event Vale won 2–1 with goals by Wilf Kirkham and Stewart Littlewood, and there was more good news after the game. It transpired that Barnsley had lost at home 4–1 to mid-table Charlton Athletic, and besides leaving them only 1 point in front of the Vale, they now had an inferior goal average. Goal average was the confusing way in which teams on the same points were separated in those days, dividing goals scored by goals conceded.

They were still in with a chance on the final day then, although Vale faced a trip to already-promoted Leeds United, who hadn't lost at home since early September, while Barnsley travelled to struggling Oldham Athletic.

Vale produced a masterful display to win 2–0, with goals by Littlewood again and Tommy Tippett. News came through that Barnsley had only drawn 2–2, so the Vale had pulled off a miraculous escape on goal average. For the record, Vale's was 0.652 whereas Barnsley's was 0.604.

GREAT ESCAPE (2)

Prior to automatic relegation from the Football League to non-league which has been in place since 1987, the bottom four teams in the Fourth Division had to apply for re-election every year. Port Vale have never finished in the bottom four in their history, but they had a narrow escape at the end of the 1979/80 season.

With two games to go the team lay in 22nd place, with Hereford United and Darlington just above them. A crucial 1–0 win at Stockport County courtesy of a Tony Sealy goal moved them above Hereford going into the last game. The last game was against Doncaster Rovers and Vale turned it on to win 3–0, their biggest victory since the previous September. The goals came from Steve Jones, a Neil Griffiths penalty and one from Russell Bromage. Darlington had been beaten 1–0 at home by Bournemouth and Hereford drew to leave Vale 'clear' at fifth from the bottom.

There was still a possible twist in the tale, though. Hereford still had one more game to play (in those days they didn't make everyone finish on the same day) and it was away at Rochdale, who were a long way adrift at the bottom despite winning their last two games. Hereford needed a three-goal margin to condemn the Vale to the bottom four and a quite a few Vale fans made the trip to Spotland to witness the drama.

Hereford took a two-goal lead in the first fifteen minutes and it seemed only a matter of time, but a great goalkeeping display by David Felgate made sure that Hereford didn't get another. Rochdale rallied to make a game of it and had a goal disallowed as well as missing a penalty. At the end of the game there was a pitch invasion by Vale supporters to cheer the home custodian off!

It all meant that Vale and Hereford were level on points and both had a negative goal difference of -14, so goals scored was the next separation criteria. Vale had scored 56 compared to Hereford's 38 so it was the Bulls who had to go cap-in-hand to the league for re-election. And to think . . . it didn't seem important at the time when Vale scored a late goal when 7–0 down at Huddersfield Town!

FESTIVAL OF BRITAIN

The 1951 Festival of Britain commemorated the centenary of the Great Exhibition of 1851 and several friendly football matches took place, many featuring foreign teams. Port Vale met FC Progrès Niedercorn of Luxembourg in May 1951 and won 4–1 in front of a crowd of 5,459. The Vale goalscorers were Len Barber (2), Alan Bennett and Stan Polk.

WHERE'S YOUR TROPHY GONE?

Port Vale have won the Football League Trophy on two occasions, and each time they had to defeat the holders on their own ground. To add spice to it, the holders on both occasions were neighbours Stoke City!

It was called the Autoglass Trophy in 1992/93 and the two sides were drawn together in the Southern semi-finals in March 1993. The clubs occupied the top two places in the Second Division at that time as well, so the intense rivalry produced an attendance of 22,254, remarkable for that stage of the competition. Stoke dominated the game, and Mark Stein missed a 12th-minute penalty, but Robin Van Der Laan became the Valiants' hero. It was in the 53rd minute when he headed home a free kick from Chris Sulley and that proved to be the only goal of the game. Vale went on to win the trophy, defeating Stockport County 2–1 at Wembley.

By the time the 2000/01 season came around, the competition was known as the LDV Vans Trophy. Again the sides met in the area semi-finals, this time the Northern area owing to their central geographical location. The Vale were drawn at home on this occasion, but after it was postponed twice, once for frost, the other for waterlogging, the Football League got a bit twitchy and insisted on the clubs playing it at Stoke's Britannia Stadium.

Vale duly obliged and won again! Cummins gave Vale the lead, but Stoke equalised to send it into extra time. In those days the golden goal rule applied, meaning the first extra-time goal won the game. As previously mentioned, a hand ball in the box meant a penalty to the Vale and Marc Bridge-Wilkinson duly ended the game fifteen minutes early! Vale went on to win the final at the Millennium Stadium against Brentford.

Both these events produced a new chant for Vale fans to sing to their rivals, to the tune of 'Chirpy Chirpy, Cheep Cheep', 'Where's your trophy gone, where's your trophy gone? Five miles away!'

HELL MONTH

Undoubtedly one of the worst months in the Vale's long history was January 1981. It began with a home draw against non-league Enfield in the third round of the FA Cup, followed by an embarrassing 3–0 defeat in the replay. That was the club's first defeat by a non-league outfit since 1937.

That was followed by a 3–0 defeat at Hartlepool United and then a 5–0 thrashing at Mansfield Town, all the goals coming in the first 39 minutes. On the final day of the month they were beaten 3–2 at home by Wimbledon and so entered February in bottom place in the Fourth Division, or 92nd in the Football League. Not a month to remember too fondly. They rallied a bit to finish nineteenth that season.

AWAY GOALS

In the days when League Cup ties were played over two legs, away goals were a common way of deciding who went through. It occurred in Vale games on four occasions, with the Vale winning two and losing two. The wins were against Bury in a first-round tie in 1984/85 (home 1–0, away 1–2) and then against Notts County in a second-round tie in 1991/92 (home 2–1, away 2–3).

The defeats were against Lincoln City in a first-round tie in 1993/94 (home 2–2, away 0–0) and old foes Tranmere Rovers in a first-round tie in 1980/81 (home 2–3, away 1–0). In all four cases, Vale played at home first.

FLOODLIGHT PIONEERS

Port Vale were one of the first English clubs to play a game under floodlights. It was actually way back in September 1886. They played a friendly against Goldenhill under an experimental electric light system, but it didn't work too well as the generator kept failing and it eventually packed up. They tried again a few days later against the same opposition and this time they got through the game, losing 3–1, but the experiment was never repeated.

They were involved in another experiment, only this time it wasn't in this country; it took place during a short tour of Holland back in May 1931. The home side were called Zwaluen, and were a team of international reserves, and they met the Vale in The Hague. Four huge arc lights were placed above each of the corners as an experiment, and that wasn't the only thing that seemed different to the Vale players. The Dutch side were constantly using substitutes as well, something the players had never experienced before, and it was over 30 years before that was adopted into the English game. Zwaluen won 2–0, but the two-game tour was a success as the Vale made a profit of £52.

A MAN OF MANY CLUBS

Scotsman Billy Barr is believed to have been the trainer at more clubs than any other, twelve in all, all between the two world wars. The full list is Kilmarnock, Third Lanark, Raith Rovers, Sheffield Wednesday, Huddersfield Town, Luton Town, Coventry City, Walsall, Swindon Town, Bristol Rovers, Exeter City and Port Vale. He left the Vale under a bit of cloud, though, as in June 1923 he sent a letter to the Football League claiming that the Vale had made illegal payments to some players during the 1921/22 season. The case went to court and Vale were fined. They hit back at Barr by accusing him of obtaining £15 by false pretences, but although he was arrested, he was subsequently acquitted.

SCORING GOALKEEPER

The only goalkeeper to have ever scored for Port Vale in a bona fide first-team game is Arthur Box. He made over 50 appearances between the Vale posts in the early part of the last century and took a penalty in March 1906. He scored, and it was the only goal of the game – against Manchester United no less! After leaving the Vale he also played for Stoke, Birmingham, Leek Victoria and Crewe Alexandra.

Billy Rowley was a Hanley-born goalkeeper who played for the Vale in the 1880s before league football came into being. He played 66 games in a variety of local competitions and scored a goal in the final of the Burslem Challenge Cup against a team called Ironbridge in March 1885. Vale were so dominant, winning 12–0, that Billy got bored during the game and joined the attack, scoring one of the goals! He moved to Stoke in 1886 and went on to play for England.

The only other custodian to come close to that feat was Mark Goodlad, who despatched a penalty in a shootout victory over Chesterfield in November 2002. The game was an LDV Vans Trophy game and it was one of the first five, not a sudden-death effort. Vale won 4–3.

NAME CHANGE

Louis Buckhalter, a Jewish Lithuanian, emigrated to Ireland in the 1890s but changed his surname by deed poll to Bookman to escape the persecution that Jews were forced to endure. He was such a good footballer that he played for Ireland on four occasions and also played for Belfast Celtic, Bradford City, West Brom, Glentoran, Shelbourne and Luton Town before joining the Vale for £250 in 1923. He made 11 senior appearances on the left wing before departing back to Ireland to play for Shelbourne once more.

Arthur Longbottom joined the Vale for £2,000 from Queens Park Rangers in May 1961 and scored on his debut against Shrewsbury Town. He changed his name by deed poll to Arthur Langley, probably because he was fed up at the jokes his name produced, but was still known as Longbottom in football circles. He left the Vale after scoring 22 goals in 60 games and later played for Millwall, Oxford United, Colchester United and Scarborough.

Colin Pluck was a defender with Watford, Morton, Stevenage, Hayes, Dover and Yeovil, and while with the latter he changed his name for family reasons to Colin Miles in 2004. It was under the latter name that he played for the Vale between 2006 and 2008.

LOCAL REFEREE

Since the early days of the Football League, it is pretty rare that a game is refereed by a local official, but it happened at Port Vale in February 2010. The match referee for the League Two home game against Barnet was Scott Mathieson from Stockport, but he injured his hamstring during the warm-up, rendering him unfit to referee. Normally the lead referee's assistant (or linesman to the majority) takes over but on this occasion, both linesmen were in their first season and therefore not allowed to referee. Attention turned to the fourth official, an experienced linesman in the form Carl Dunn from Chesterton, a mere 5 miles from Vale Park. He too had never refereed a league game, but was more experienced and after having the go-ahead from referee assessor Roger Milford, took over the whistle to referee his 'local' team!

In the event there was no controversy as Barnet won 2–0. No doubt the Londoners would have been ready to schedule a complaint had the Vale won with a dodgy penalty!

TOP SCORER FOR TWO CLUBS

When Cyril Done topped the Vale scoring charts in the 1954/55 season, he achieved a feat that had never happened before or since – he finished that season as the leading scorer for two clubs, and on both occasions had scored twice as many as the next player on the list! He notched 13 for the Vale, with Basil Hayward and Stan Smith the next on the list who had 6 league goals each. At Tranmere Cyril scored 15 league goals before leaving to join the Vale halfway through the season, but no one else managed more than 6 goals for the Rovers!

STEWART LITTLEWOOD: THE GOALSCORING ENIGMA

Stewart was a bit of a goalscoring enigma, with a great scoring record, 35 goals in just 54 games, but was always in and out of the side. He originally joined the Vale in November 1926 and scored 8 goals in his first 3 reserve games, which resulted in a call-up to the first team. He promptly scored twice in a 2–1 win at Clapton Orient, but returned to the reserves when Wilf Kirkham was fit.

In the 1927/28 campaign, he scored a remarkable 55 goals in just 33 reserve team games plus 7 goals in 7 games for the first team. In 1928/29 he scored 9 goals in 10 games for the first team before being transferred to Oldham Athletic in exchange for Albert Pynegar plus £1,500 in January 1929. Supporters were not happy, because his record stood out. He continued in the same vein at Oldham with 48 goals in 77 games, but when the Vale were lying 5th in the Second Division in March 1931 they re-signed Stewart for a club record fee of around £4,000.

Unfortunately injuries limited his appearances over the next 18 months, but then Stewart went down in Port Vale history by scoring 6 goals in one game, the most by any player. His red-letter day arrived in September 1932 against Chesterfield in a Second Division game played at the Old Recreation Ground in Hanley. Vale won 9–1, still a club record victory.

Stewart opened the scoring after 6 minutes and Chesterfield promptly equalised, but he completed his hat-trick in the first half as Vale led 4–1 at the interval and then scored three more between the 51st and 57th minutes. Wilf Kirkham (2) and Bob Morton completed the scoring. It was also a record at the time for a player to score so many against his previous club, Stewart having been a junior with Chesterfield.

Again injuries limited his involvement and he only managed 13 games that season (with 10 goals) and he left at the end of it, joining Bournemouth.

DOUBLE EMBARRASSMENT

In the 2003/04 season Port Vale achieved an unwanted Football League record, which is unlikely ever to be beaten. They managed to lose to the same non-league club twice in the same season! For a six-year period, LDV, the sponsors of the trophy for lower division teams, allowed eight non-league clubs to enter. In the second round the Vale were drawn away to Scarborough, then of the Conference, and lost 2–1. Later the same season, the two teams were paired in the second round of the FA Cup, this time at Vale Park. Again Scarborough triumphed, this time 1–0.

NATIONAL VISITORS

The first overseas visitors to play Port Vale were a team of Canadian football players on tour in 1891. They had a successful tour in 1888 but it didn't go so well for them three years later, losing 31 out of a remarkably long 59-game tour lasting almost six months! Burslem Port Vale weren't a league side when the Canadians turned up for a friendly in December 1891 at the Athletic Ground in Cobridge. Vale won 2–0 thanks to goals from Scarratt and Pimlott and the game ended with a fierce argument in the dressing room after the Canadians had a man sent off.

Port Vale have twice played home friendlies against a bona fide national team. The first occasion was in October 1961 when Czechoslovakia sent their full side over as a goodwill gesture after the Vale toured there the previous year. The Czechs were a good side in those days, and had just lost 3–2 to Scotland, only their second defeat in 11 games. The teams lined up as follows:

Port Vale – Hancock, Whalley, Sproson, Ford, Nicholson, Miles, Jackson, Poole, Llewellyn, Steele, Longbottom
Czechoslovakia – Jindra, Hledik, Tichy, Pluskai, Poplukar, Bubernik, Vacenovsky, Scherer, Kucera, Kvasnak, Masek

The crowd of 22,895 saw the visitors win 3–1, although Bert Llewellyn did equalise for the Vale with just over a quarter of an hour to go. The Czechs went on to prove how good they were by reaching the World Cup final just eight months later, losing 3–1 to Brazil in Chile. Five of the players in the team that played at the Vale were in their final line-up.

The other international visitors were Zimbabwe and that was a much more low-key affair in August 1983. It was a pre-season friendly, and a crowd of only 1,620 saw the Vale win 2–1. Their goalscorers were Jim Steel and Wayne Cegielski.

YORKSHIRE CRICKETERS

What links famous Yorkshire and England cricketers Brian Close and David Bairstow with Port Vale? Well, early in their careers they also played a bit of football with Bradford City and both appeared at Vale Park. In fact Brian's last ever Football League game was at Vale Park in December 1952 when he limped off with a serious knee injury that also threatened his promising cricket career, having three years earlier become the youngest ever Englishman to play Test cricket. After that he decided to pack the football side of his career in.

David Bairstow also tried to combine both sports in his career and appeared at the Vale as a substitute in February 1972. Soon after, he too decided to stick to the small red ball game.

HIGHS AND LOWS

The highest position that Port Vale have ever finished in is 5th in the old Second Division in the 1930/31 season. The highest position the club have ever held during the season is top of the Second Division, in September 1893, when the club had won their first 7 games, and in November 1933 when they eventually finished 8th.

The lowest position the club have ever finished in is 20th in the old Fourth Division in the 1979/80 season, when goals scored kept them out of the bottom four. Since the Football League has comprised 92 clubs, the Vale have been bottom of the pile mid-season in the Septembers of 1967, 1968, 1979, 1980 and January 1981.

TOP DOGS

If you ask Port Vale fans they already know that they are the top dogs in the area, but it has been official on a number of occasions. The Vale have been a division above their local rivals Stoke City on five occasions, 1926/27, 1990/91, 1991/92, 1998/99 and 1999/2000. When the teams have been in the same division, the Vale have finished higher seven times, in 1924/25, 1925/26, 1930/31, 1955/56, 1989/90, 1996/97 and 1997/98. So, as regards bragging rights, the Vale were top dogs for three successive years in the Roaring Twenties, and again for seven seasons out of eleven between 1989 and 2000.

BACK TO THE LEAGUE
THANKS TO A CHARLIE

Port Vale had resigned from the Football League due to financial difficulties in 1907, but had regrouped and were ready to try again after the First World War had ended in 1918. The League announced that they would be expanding the competition from 40 clubs to 44 for the 1919/20 season and with Glossop North End having failed re-election in 1915, the last season of the league before the war, it meant that five new clubs were to be admitted.

Vale's neighbours Stoke had been re-elected instead of Glossop in 1915 until hostilities suspended the League so it was only fair to let them have one of the places. As former League members, the Vale thought they were a certainty for one of the other four, but when the voting was announced in March 1919 it read as follows; Coventry City 35, West Ham 32, South Shields 28, Rotherham County 28, Port Vale 27, Southport 7, Rochdale 7 and Chesterfield 0. So they missed out by one vote.

That wasn't the end of the drama, though. A former player at Second Division Leeds City, Charlie Copeland, wrote to the Football League alleging that the club had made illegal payments to players during the war leagues, when guest players had featured. It is believed he took this action after being refused a pay rise. The League were obliged to investigate but Leeds continually refused to let anyone see their accounts. As pressure mounted in October 1919, Leeds manager Herbert Chapman set fire to the books!

Despite nothing ever being proved then, Leeds were expelled from the League and Chapman was banned for life. He later got this rescinded by saying that he was working in munitions when it was supposed to have happened and went on to have success with Huddersfield Town and Arsenal, who both won a hat-trick of league titles. His bust is in the Arsenal entrance hall to the Emirates Stadium.

This meant that the Second Division was a club short and because they only missed out by one vote previously, Port Vale were duly asked to take over their fixtures on 13 October 1919, despite a late bid from Tranmere Rovers.

Leeds had played eight games, earning 10 points, and the Vale were given that record. Their main problem was getting a team together: they only had five days to prepare for their first match as players had to be registered properly with the Football League. In the event they lost 2–0 at South Shields, but at least they were back in the Football League! Thank you Charlie Copeland.

CHAMPIONS OF GREAT BRITAIN

It's not often that you hear the phrase, 'Port Vale are the Champions of Great Britain.' It did happen though, five times to be exact, when the Port Vale Supporters Club won the National Federation of Supporters' Clubs football quiz competition. All the questions came from the *Rothmans Football Yearbook*, and they won it in 1975, 1977, 1978, 1980 and 1981, defeating teams from as far apart as Gravesend in Kent, and Hamilton in Scotland. It could have been even better, because although undefeated in 1976, the team withdrew in protest over the football club's sale of Brian Horton to Brighton.

The proud unbeaten record came to an end against Leeds United in 1979, but they bounced back to take the title again for another two years. After that, defeats against Wrexham and Leeds again in the 1984 final precipitated 'retirement' although the competition continued for many years afterwards.

HAT-TRICKS

Since competitive football began, no less than 106 hat-tricks have been scored in Vale colours – one 6, two 5s, sixteen 4s and 87 threesomes.

Stewart Littlewood was the man who notched the six against Chesterfield when they were beaten 9–1 in September 1932.

The fives were scored by Frank Watkin against Rotherham in February 1930 (7–1), and Andy Jones, who scored five against Newport County in May 1987 (6–1).

The man who has notched the most hat-tricks is the club record scorer Wilf Kirkham, who managed 13 altogether, and he is way ahead of the next on the list, Tom Nolan and Darren Beckford who each scored five.

The fastest hat-trick was scored by Fred Mitcheson in just under three minutes of a 4–0 victory over Plymouth Argyle in April 1934. It was only his second appearance as well!

The youngest hat-trick scorer is Ronnie Allen, who was 18 years and 234 days old when he scored a threesome in a remarkable 6–4 victory over Aldershot in September 1947.

Cliff Pinchbeck is the only Vale player to mark his debut with a hat-trick. He cost £3,500 from Brighton in September 1949 and two days later scored a hat-trick in a 4–0 win over Millwall.

Andy Jones deserves a mention, as his three hat-tricks comprised a three, a four and a five!

Striker Bert Llewellyn is the only one known to have scored a hat-trick of headers, in a 3–1 FA Cup third-round victory over Northampton in January 1962.

Bobby Gough managed to score a hat-trick in a Vale side that was still beaten by four clear goals! His threesome came at Shrewsbury Town in September 1970 but Vale still lost 7–3.

Strangely the last five hat-tricks for the club have all been scored away from home. The last man to score one at Vale Park is Martin Foyle who scored three against Hartlepool in the first round of the FA Cup in a 6–0 win in November 1994.

TESTIMONIALS

Testimonial games are usually knock-about affairs, with guest players, dodgy penalties and all sorts of things going on. There can't have been many that have ended goalless though, but that is exactly what happened in August 1979. It was John Brodie's testimonial, and the opposition were Everton but the game resulted in a 0–0 draw! Certainly a far cry from Ray Walker's testimonial in May 1997 when Leicester City won 8–6!

Testimonials are rarer these days as players never seem to stay long enough to earn one, but there were quite a few when the Vale's great experienced team of the 1990s began to be broken up. From a player's point of view, the trick was to get Vale fan Robbie Williams to play, as he always wanted to represent his beloved club, and this would set the turnstiles clicking furiously as his musical career took off.

Dean Glover was the first to benefit in May 1998, when Robbie scored a penalty and was then sent off against Aston Villa in front of over 5,000. It's fair to say the red card was probably pre-planned for crowd entertainment. A year later he was back again for Neil Aspin's testimonial and 6,000 turned up for a 5–3 win over Leicester City, also including another Williams strike.

Things moved up a notch in May 2001 though, and people came from all over the country to see Robbie turn out in Martin Foyle's testimonial. The queues were enormous and it is estimated that over 12,000 saw Robbie score another penalty, this time against Manchester City. Jonathan Wilkes also played in that game.

UPROAR AT UNKNOWNS

When the Vale drew Manchester United in the second round of the Coca-Cola Cup in September 1994, the fans were excited at the prospect of seeing so many big names playing at Vale Park in the first leg. Peter Schmeichel, Steve Bruce, Eric Cantona, Gary Pallister, Paul Ince and Mark Hughes were all regulars in their Premier League side, but there was uproar from the 18,000 crowd when none of those were in the side that night. Instead, the crowd were treated to a load of youngsters who were virtually unknown in those days, and this was the first time that a team had deliberately fielded what was really a reserve side in a cup tie. Unknowns called Gary Neville, David Beckham, Paul Scholes, Nicky Butt and Keith Gillespie wore the red shirts that night, but little did the crowd know what players they were going to become!

United still won 2–1 with two goals by Paul Scholes, the first of his illustrious career, while Beckham was making the first start of his career. The second leg ended 2–0 in United's favour.

HEAVY DEFEATS ABOUND

Port Vale had a good season in 1972/73. They were in the Third Division at the time, and eventually finished 6th, but that was in the days before the play-offs. What was unusual was that they finished the season with a -13 goal difference, and purely for away games it was a staggering -33!

The reason was that whenever they did lose, it was invariably a heavy defeat. They lost 7–0 at Rotherham, 5–0 at Brentford, Southend and Wrexham, 4–0 at Bournemouth and 4–1 at Bristol Rovers. That's 30 goals conceded in 6 games, but they only conceded 18 in the other 17 away games!

SENDINGS OFF

Sendings off are the bane of a footballer's life. Port Vale have had their fair share over the years which have produced a few stories on their way. The first Vale player to be sent off was goalkeeper John Davis in May 1890. The rules had only recently been changed to allow sendings off and John took umbrage after being kicked in the face and retaliated in a 'friendly' against Walsall Town Swifts. Vale still won 5–1 though.

The most the club have ever had sent off in a particular season is 7, which they 'achieved' in 1974/75 and again in 2001/02. In the former campaign the team received two red cards in one game for the first time, in a controversial 3–1 defeat at Huddersfield Town in March 1975. Full-back Neil Griffiths was the first to go, but then the other full-back, John Brodie, followed suit. What was unusual about Brodie's dismissal was that while committing what was deemed a foul tackle he managed to break his own leg, and so received the red card in his face while departing the field of play on a stretcher! A far cry from years gone by, as between 1919 and 1947 the club only had two players sent off altogether.

The club have only done the 'double' of two dismissals in a game on one other occasion, a Littlewoods Cup tie at home to Northampton Town in August 1987. Ray Walker and Paul Smith both did the walk of shame that night, but Northampton also had two players sent off, and the four dismissals still constitute a League Cup record.

The individual serial offender at the top of the club's disciplinary chart is full-back Jason Talbot who managed 5 red cards within just 33 appearances between 2005 and 2007. Midfielder Tommy Widdrington holds a couple of unusual red card records. After being sent off playing for Southampton at the Vale in an FA Cup tie in January 1994, he became the first man to be sent off both for and against the Vale in May 1999 when he was on loan at Port Vale. That indiscretion occurred on the final day of the season at Bury. He also managed to pick up two red cards in less than a minute! Following that sending off at Bury, he then joined the Vale on a permanent basis. He had to serve a suspension first, but in his first game back at Birmingham City, he was again red carded just 45 seconds into the game for a waist-high tackle on Gary Rowett!

Striker Bernie Slaven is the only Vale player to mark his debut for the club by being red-carded. That was in March 1993 when he was sent packing for violent conduct. Vale still won 1–0, though.

GROUNDS

The Vale have played home games on seven different grounds altogether.

1876–81	Limekiln Lane
1881–4	Westport Meadows
1884–6	Moorland Road
1886–1913	Athletic Ground
1913–50	Old Recreation Ground
1950 – date	Vale Park

NB: two home games were also played at the Victoria Ground in the 1950/51 season.

COMEDY GOALKEEPER

Many Port Vale fans will admit to having seen a comedian play in goal for their side over the years, but it really did happen in the late 1960s. Liverpool-born Mick Lawton was a promising schoolboy footballer and he responded to a magazine advert in which Sir Stanley Matthews no less was advertising for young players to come to Port Vale for a trial. That was Sir Stan's blueprint for the future for Port Vale in 1965 and Mick joined what was a large throng from far and wide. He progressed through the youth team and made four appearances for the reserves, but when it came to the make-or-break time to become a professional, he was released.

He then gave up football, changed his name to Mick Miller, and started to work at Pontins. He later became well known on TV on *The Comedians* and often referred to his time between the posts at the Vale.

'They used to call me the Cat,' he said, 'because I used to give the back four kittens!'

He still works as a comedian nowadays and often returns to the Vale for after dinner functions, the last of which was in late 2009.

SIMPLY THE BEST

John Rudge should go down in Vale history as their greatest ever manager because he achieved a unique feat at the club – he took them to promotion to the second tier of English football twice. It's fair to say that very few Vale supporters had heard of him when he was appointed coach to John McGrath in January 1980. He had only been a journeyman footballer with Huddersfield Town (where he cleaned the boots of Denis Law!) Carlisle United, Torquay United, Bristol Rovers and Bournemouth, and was coaching at Torquay before joining the Vale.

At the time the Vale were at a very low ebb and finished that season in the lowest position in their history, 20th in Division Four. The two Johns made a good combination, McGrath being the more extrovert with the media while Rudge just got on with his job quietly behind the scenes. They put together a promotion-winning outfit in the 1982/83 season, but then things began to go wrong the following campaign. Player unrest and a run of eighteen games without a win took their toll. Towards the end of that run Vale lost 7–0 at Burnley, being 7 down after 49 minutes, and after a 1–0 home defeat by Gillingham, McGrath was sacked with Rudge taking temporary charge.

It was a thankless task to try to avoid relegation, the team having only 6 points at Christmas, but a revival that produced five home wins out of six meant that Rudge was appointed manager on a permanent basis in March 1984. He put together a side good enough to get promoted from the Fourth Division in 1985/86 but after the sale of Andy Jones for a club record £350,000 in 1987, the club had a bad run and went twelve games without a league victory. It was widely rumoured that a managerial change was imminent had the club lost to non-league Macclesfield Town in the FA Cup, but they won 1–0. The whole club hit the headlines in January 1988 when they knocked Terry Venables' Spurs side out of the FA Cup and have never really looked back since.

Finances enabled Rudge to put together a better team and in 1988/89 they achieved the unthinkable by getting promoted to Division Two after an absence of 32 years. They had to do it via the play-offs, in those days two-legged affairs, and no-one present will forget the day Bristol Rovers, ironically Rudge's old club, were beaten at Vale Park in June 1989.

Vale held their own in the Second Division for a couple of years before being relegated in 1992 but then were only thwarted of an immediate return by defeat in the play-off final at Wembley against West Brom. They had the 'consolation' prize of the Autoglass Trophy though – another unforgettable experience under the twin towers.

It was automatic promotion in 1993/94 and Rudge piloted the team to become comfortable in what is now called the Championship. They reached the Anglo–Italian Cup final at Wembley in 1996 and then a year later had the temerity to finish 8th in the table, the club's best for 63 years, just 4 points short of a place in the play-offs to get into the Premier League. Now that *would* have been something!

As often happens to smaller clubs at that level, it got difficult to sustain and after a near miss at relegation in 1998, the club embarked in a run of eleven defeats from fourteen games the following season. In January 1999 the axe fell on the Vale's longest-serving manager after a 1–0 defeat against Swindon Town, ending a remarkable 843 games in charge. Manchester United manager Alex Ferguson (not then a Sir) summed it up succinctly, saying, 'Every Port Vale fan should go down on their knees and thank the Lord for John Rudge.'

The supporters protested to no avail, and held a dinner in his honour. He never took up another managerial appointment and became director of football at rivals Stoke City, a position he still holds.

Rudge career highlights
Promotion to Division Three 1986
Promotion to Division Two 1989, 1994
Finished 8th Division Two 1997
Autoglass Trophy winners 1993
Anglo–Italian Cup runners–up 1996

To add to the basic facts, you can factor in FA Cup wins over top division sides including Tottenham Hotspur, Everton and Derby County, five victories over neighbours Stoke City and making the Vale the number one club in the Potteries for a spell. Not a bad time to have been a Vale fan.

GIANT-KILLING

Over the years Port Vale have had many giant-killings in cup competitions. Altogether they have defeated seven top-flight sides.

1897/98
FA Cup first round, Burslem Port Vale 2 Sheffield United 1 (after a 1–1 draw)

Vale were in the Midland League in those days and faced little chance away to the First Division leaders (and eventual champions) Sheffield United. Over 14,000 turned up to see the expected slaughter but Ted McDonald gave Vale the lead and only a debatable penalty saw the tie go to a replay.

Vale turned down £250 to stage the game at Bramall Lane and took the lead at Cobridge after 2 minutes thanks to Dick Evans. United equalised 8 minutes from the end to send the game into extra time. United threw everything at Vale and even their goalkeeper, the legendary England International William 'Fatty' Foulke (he was over 20 stone, hence the nickname), joined in their attacks. Foulke was hopelessly out of position when Billy Heames raced half of the length of the pitch and passed to Lucien Boullemier who scored the winner!

Vale – Birchenough, Clare, Spilsbury, Boullemier, Beech, McDonald, R. Evans, J. Evans, Simpson, Peake, Heames

1935/36

FA Cup third round, Port Vale 2 Sunderland 0
(after a 2–2 draw)

Sunderland were the runaway First Division leaders (and eventual champions) whereas the Vale were next to bottom of the Second Division. Vale had conceded 48 goals in twelve away games that season but remarkably held on for a 2–2 draw thanks to a late equaliser from Arthur Caldwell.

The replay was expected to go Sunderland's way, but Vale's fighting spirit kicked in and they were 2–0 up in the replay after just 18 minutes thanks to goals by George Stabb and Trevor Rhodes. That was how it stayed to the euphoria of the Old Recreation ground crowd of 16,677.

Vale – Potts, Welsh, Vickers, Curley, Griffiths, Jones, Johnson, Rhodes, Baker, Stabb, Caldwell

1953/54

FA Cup fourth round, Cardiff City 0 Port Vale 2

Vale were riding high at the top of the Third Division (North) while Cardiff were a mid-table First Division side. Vale's famed Iron Curtain defence had only conceded 12 goals in thirty-one games that season, and they did the business again, with yet another clean sheet. Ken Griffiths and Albert Leake scored the Vale goals and Cardiff were so impressed with winger Colin Askey that they offered £25,000 to sign him. When that was rebuffed they offered a blank cheque! That too was rebuffed!

Vale – King, Turner, Potts, Mullard, Cheadle, Sproson, Askey, Leake, Hayward, Griffiths, Cunliffe

1953/54
FA Cup fifth round, Port Vale 2 Blackpool 0

A full house of 42,000 (and a further 8,000 locked outside) crammed into Vale Park to see the FA Cup holders Blackpool, Stanley Matthews and all. The pitch resembled a mud bath and Vale adapted far better to the conditions; it was Albert Leake who scored twice early on to set the ground rocking. Again it was the Iron Curtain that kept things tight at the back and it was the Vale who swept into the quarter-finals of the competition for the only time in their history. The Blackpool team contained Jackie Mudie and Len Stephenson, both of whom went on to play for the Vale in future years.

Vale – King, Turner, Potts, Mullard, Cheadle, Sproson, Askey, Leake, Hayward, Griffiths, Cunliffe

1963/64
FA Cup third round, Birmingham City 1 Port Vale 2

Birmingham were battling against relegation from the top flight but were still expected to beat a Vale side who were just below halfway in the Third Division. Over 3,000 Vale fans made the trip to St Andrews and cheered their heads off as the Vale came away with a surprise 2–1 victory. Stalwart Roy Sproson and Jackie Mudie, who had been on the wrong end of a Vale giant-killing ten years previously, scored the goals that mattered.

Vale – Hancock, Whalley, Wilson, Rawlings, Nicholson, Sproson, Rowland, Steele, Richards, Mudie, Smith

1987/88
FA Cup fourth round, Port Vale 2 Tottenham Hotspur 1

Spurs were managed by Terry Venables and having reached the final the previous year were expected to easily beat a Vale side struggling in the lower reaches of the Third Division. Football pundit Jimmy Greaves even said on TV that Spurs' biggest problem would be finding the ground! A heavy pitch negated Spurs 'fancy dans' and Vale revelled in the conditions, taking a 2–0 lead in the first 25 minutes. A Ray Walker cracker and one from Phil Sproson did the damage and they hung on in the second half despite Neil 'Razor' Ruddock pulling a goal back. It was Vale's first starring role on *Match of the Day*, and the game was broadcast live in Scandinavia! That really did put the Vale on the map.

Vale – Grew, Steggles, Hughes, Walker, Hazell, Sproson, Ford, Earle, Riley, Beckford (Finney), Cole

1989/90
FA Cup third round, Derby County 2 Port Vale 3 (after a 1–1 draw)

Vale went into this game as a mid–table Second Division side, and were still confident going into the replay despite having drawn at home in the first game. An own goal put Vale in front and after an equaliser from Ramage, further strikes from Ray Walker and Nicky Cross put them 3–1 ahead. When it was 2–1 Vale were under the cosh a bit and full-back Darren Hughes picked the ball up on the edge of his own area and raced towards the Derby goal. No-one could catch him, and he simply squared it to Nicky Cross who gleefully made it 3–1. County pulled one back near the end but Vale hung on for a magnificent win. It was only the second time that Peter Shilton had conceded three goals that season.

Vale – Grew, Mills, Hughes, Walker, Aspin, Glover, Porter, Earle, Cross, Beckford, Jeffers

1995/96
FA Cup fourth round, Port Vale 2 Everton 1
(after a 1–1 draw)

Everton were the cup holders and were 8th in the Premier League whereas the Vale were 21st in Division One, albeit with games in hand due to their cup run. In the first game Vale had equalised in the final minute through Ian Bogie. In the second, Vale turned on one of their best ever displays and took the lead through Ian Bogie, although Graham Stuart levelled matters before half time. Jon McCarthy scored the winner in the second half to send the crowd into raptures. It is the only time so far that the Vale have beaten a Premier League club in competitive action.

Vale – Musselwhite, Hill, Tankard, Bogie, Griffiths, Aspin, McCarthy, Porter, Foyle, Naylor, Guppy (Walker)

TOP TEN SALES

Arguably the best spell in the club's history came during the 1990s and it comes as no surprise that the majority of large transfer fees received were during that period.

£2,000,000 Gareth Ainsworth to Wimbledon, October 1998
£1,500,000 Jon McCarthy to Birmingham City,
    September 1997
£1,000,000 Ian Taylor to Sheffield Wednesday, August 1994
£1,000,000 Lee Mills to Bradford City, August 1997
£1,000,000 Anthony Gardner to Tottenham Hotspur,
    January 2000
★£950,000 Steve Guppy to Leicester City, February 1997
£925,000 Darren Beckford to Norwich City, June 1991
£775,000 Robbie Earle to Wimbledon, June 1991

£500,000 Dave Brammer to Crewe Alex, August 2001
£350,000 Andy Jones to Charlton Athletic, August 1987

★ – including £100,000 from add-on clauses.

TOP TEN BUYS

Once again, the club's best period of the 1990s coincides with when they made their most expensive purchases:

£500,000 Gareth Ainsworth from Lincoln City,
    September 1997
£500,000 Dave Brammer from Wrexham, March 1999
£450,000 Jon McCarthy from York City, July 1995
£375,000 Martin Foyle from Oxford United, June 1991
£375,000 Marcus Bent from Crystal Palace, January 1999
£310,000 Peter Swan from Hull City, August 1991
£300,000 Peter Beadle from Bristol Rovers, August 1998
£225,000 Lee Glover from Nottingham Forest, July 1994
£225,000 Steve Guppy from Newcastle United,
    November 1994
£200,000 Dean Glover from Middlesbrough, February 1989

'WHITE' BOY

Just how did a local boy from Staffordshire become Port Vale's most capped player – for Trinidad & Tobago? A rags to riches story if ever there was one.

Chris Birchall is from Stone in Staffordshire and first joined the Vale when he was just 9 years old, rising through all of their junior sides to make the first team. He was only 17 when he made his debut, at Charlton in the League Cup in 2001. He continued to progress, having his best season in 2004/05, scoring 7 goals in 39 appearances on the right-hand side of midfield, also winning the club's Young Player of the Year Award.

It was towards the end of that season, when a chance remark in a home game against Wrexham, saw his life change forever. While there was a lull in play, Wrexham's giant central defender Dennis Lawrence marched towards Chris, seemingly on a mission. As Chris thought he was about to get his face rearranged, Dennis merely said, 'I hear you have got some Trini blood in you?' Chris's mother had indeed been born in Port of Spain, the capital of Trinidad, during a family holiday, and this fact had found its way to the Trinidad FA. Chris answered yes, and Dennis said that the Trinidad FA wanted to have a word with him.

He flew out in May 2005 to Trinidad, a place he had never visited before and caused quite a stir during a warm-up game. Being as pure as the driven snow in appearance, he soon gained the nickname 'White Boy' and was also known as 'Me Mum', as that is how he began every interview. He made his debut against Bermuda in a friendly and became the first white player to represent Trinidad & Tobago for over 60 years. He did well enough in central midfield to hold down a regular place and was soon part of their World Cup qualifying campaign. He scored a vital goal in a play-off draw with Bahrain and was part of the team that won 1–0 away to clinch a place in the final stages in Germany for the 2006 tournament. More publicity came his way as they were then drawn in England's group. Chris performed well in the three group games, and it became quite obvious that the Vale were unlikely to be able to hang on to his services.

Chris had just managed to become the Vale's most capped international with 22 appearances when he was signed by Coventry City for £300,000, ironically by a man later to become the Vale's manager, Micky Adams. He has since played for St Mirren, Carlisle United, Brighton and his present club LA Galaxy. One of his team–mates is David Beckham and he lives in an exclusive area on the west coast of America. Not bad for a young lad from Stone!

THE INTERNATIONAL SET

The players who have won international caps while playing for Port Vale are as follows:

Chris Birchall	(Trinidad & Tobago)	(2005/06)	22
Tony Rougier	(Trinidad & Tobago)	(1999/00)	20
Sammy Morgan	(N. Ireland)	(1972/73)	7
George Abbey	(Nigeria)	(2004/06)	6
Teddy Peers	(Wales)	(1922/23)	4
Eamon O'Keefe	(Republic of Ireland)	(1984/85)	4
Jon McCarthy	(N. Ireland)	(1996/97)	4
Billy Bingham	(N. Ireland)	(1963/64)	3
Andy Jones	(Wales)	(1987)	3
★ David Healy	(N. Ireland)	(2000)	2
James Lawrie	(N. Ireland)	(2009/10)	2
★ Neville Southall	(Wales)	(1983)	1

★ on loan at the Vale when they won their caps.

COMMON OPPONENTS

Which team have the Vale met most often during their long history? The club in question is none other than Barnsley, who have provided the opposition for exactly 100 Football League games. Add to it a further 9 cup ties and the total of 109 is comfortably ahead of anyone else. The next on the list is the oldest club in the Football League, Notts County, who have opposed the Vale on 97 occasions, 86 of them in league combat.

ONLY SCORED v WREXHAM

John Brodie was a dependable full-back, who went about his job to the best of his abilities. Altogether he made 193 senior appearances between 1971 and 1977. What made him stand out was the fact that he scored just three goals in those six years, and all were against Wrexham! What's more they were all in one-goal victories. His first was in September 1971 when the Vale won 2–1 at the Racecourse Ground and then he followed that with the only goal of the game in a second-round FA Cup tie the following season at Vale Park. He completed the set in October 1973, at the Vale again, with the only goal of the game!

CHRISTMAS DAY

Today's players and fans would never stand for it, but league games regularly took place on Christmas Day. It wasn't always a local derby either, and the return match was usually played a day later, on Boxing Day. Back in December 1928, Port Vale played a Second Division game at Middlesbrough on

Christmas Day, losing 5–1. They played the return the next afternoon and lost 3–2. Nine players played in both games, and with transport being far less salubrious than nowadays (no motorways for a start), it's fair to say that in those days players really did have it rough over the Christmas period.

The Vale always had more beatings than victories on Christmas Day, and travelling away they have been thumped 6–2 at Grimsby (1888), 5–0 at Lincoln (1890), 7–0 at Woolwich Arsenal (1894), and 7–0 at Leicester (1924). The best win the Vale had on the festive afternoon was a 5–0 thrashing of Brighton in 1947.

At Christmas 1950, Vale Park was unfit so the club asked to borrow Stoke City's Victoria Ground for their home game against Bristol Rovers. It finished 0–0. Crowds were always very good, and 15,322 saw a 1–0 win over Chester in 1953, but that was the last home game played by the Vale on Christmas Day.

A few years later, though, public enthusiasm was beginning to wane for games on that day, and with public transport becoming scarcer as more companies closed down for the holiday period, it was decided by the Football League to abandon the policy. The last full programme on Christmas Day was in 1957, and the Vale lost 1–0 at Coventry City.

THE OLD 'UNS

The oldest player to play for the Vale first team is Tom Holford, one of the most loyal servants the club ever had. He was a player, manager, scout and trainer, and had retired as a player a couple of years before being asked to play during an injury crisis in March 1924. He played a couple of games against Derby County as a half-back (defensive midfield in the modern parlance), the second of which was on 5 April 1924. That made Tom the grand old age of 46 years and 68 days.

The second oldest was another loyal servant, Roy Sproson, who brought the curtain down on a 22-year playing career with his 836th appearance against Rotherham United on 8 May 1972 aged 41 years and 230 days.

Arthur Bridgett was 41 years and 121 days old when he made his final bow on 9 February 1924 against Bristol City.

Alan Oakes became the oldest Vale player to make his debut for the club when he answered an injury crisis in October 1983. The former Manchester City star was a coach at the club at the time but filled in for a 1–0 home defeat against Plymouth Argyle at the age of 41 years and 60 days.

The oldest man to play in any Vale game is goalkeeper Kevin Poole, who came on as a substitute for Burton Albion at Vale Park on 19 January 2010. He was aged 46 years 182 days at the time.

FA CUP SEMIS

The furthest Port Vale have got in the FA Cup was in the record-breaking 1953/54 season when as a Third Division (North) side they reached the semi-finals.

First round, 21 November 1953 Darlington (A) 3–1, Att. 10,700

The Vale were already running away with the league having won fifteen of their twenty games so far, conceding just 7 goals in that time. They had already won at Darlington 3–0 in the league and did a similar job on this occasion. Goals from Albert Leake, Basil Hayward and Dickie Cunliffe meant a 3–1 victory.

Second round, 12 December 1953 Southport (A) 1–1, Att. 12,529

A very difficult game against a fellow Third Division team. Basil Hayward scored the goal to make sure the game went to a replay.

Second-round replay, 14 December 1953 Southport (H) 2–0, Att. 13,024

Again a difficult game, played in the afternoon just two days after the original tie in the days before floodlights. Colin Askey and Basil Hayward did the damage.

Third round, 9 January 1954 Queens Park Rangers (A) 1–0, Att. 17,474

A visit to a struggling Third Division (South) outfit presented no obstacle to a Vale side despite the wet and windy conditions. Mind you, the Vale did look a bit strange – they wore a strip of red and white striped shirts, the colours of neighbours Stoke City! They were backed by a large following of supporters who travelled by train, having paid 22s 6d (£1.12) for the privilege. Albert Leake scored the only goal of the game.

Fourth round, 30 January 1954 Cardiff City (A) 2–0, Att. 27,295

By now the Vale were becoming well known in the media, but this was to be their stiffest test so far. Cardiff were halfway up the First Division and had quite a few internationals in their line up, including Welsh striker Trevor Ford. Vale's famed 'Iron Curtain' defence never gave them a sniff, though, and goals by Ken Griffiths and Albert Leake made it a successful afternoon.

Fifth round, 20 February 1954 Blackpool (H) 2–0, Att. 42,000

This was one of the biggest games the Vale have ever staged, against the cup holders who included Stanley Matthews and six other internationals in their line-up. Stoke offered the use of their ground, but Vale preferred to play it at home and were rewarded with a full house of 42,000 with 8,000 more locked outside. The pitch was very muddy, but Vale adapted to the conditions far better and were soon 2–0 ahead thanks to a brace by Albert Leake. That was how it stayed and the Vale were in the quarter-finals for the first time ever.

Sixth round, 13 March 1954 Leyton Orient (A) 1–0, Att. 31,000

Only one Third Division team had ever reached the FA Cup semi-finals before, Millwall in 1937, and by pitting the only two Third Division survivors together it was going to happen again this year. Around 8,000 Vale supporters travelled as cup fever enveloped the whole club and the game was featured on BBC's *Match of the Day*, which in those days was a radio programme. Albert Leake made sure the fairytale continued with the only goal of the game.

Semi-final, 27 March 1954 (at Villa Park) West Brom 1–2, Att. 68,221

Of course the clamour for tickets went berserk. They were sold at first inside the ground for a reserve game, which meant that the might of Mossley triggered an attendance of 30,000, ironically higher than any league game that season! A fleet of over 100 coaches and 14 special trains ferried them all down to Villa Park for a tie against the First Division leaders West Bromwich Albion and it was a case of 'let battle commence'. Vale had to make a team change for the first time in the run – Ken Griffiths was injured and replaced by Derek Tomkinson.

Vale played their usual game in the first half, the Iron Curtain stood firm and the unthinkable seemed on when Albert Leake gave them an interval lead in the 40th minute. West Brom equalised in the 62nd minute when a long cross from the right brushed Tommy Cheadle's head as he attempted to clear, but it nestled in the corner of the net. At 1–1 thoughts turned to a possible replay, which would be held at Stoke.

It was not to be, though, as 8 minutes later a challenge by Cheadle on George Lee was deemed to be a penalty despite being seemingly outside the area. The man entrusted to take the penalty was none other than Ronnie Allen, a former Vale player who was born in Stoke-on-Trent. He scored. Vale then had a goal by Leake disallowed for offside and it all ended in tears. At least they had the consolation of winning the Third Division (North) Championship.

The Vale team right up to the semi-finals was:
King, Turner, Potts, Mullard, Cheadle, Sproson, Askey, Leake, Hayward, Griffiths, Cunliffe.
In the semi-final Tomkinson replaced Griffiths.

DESTROYED BY RYAN WILSON

When the Vale reached the third round of the FA Youth Cup in the 1989/90 season, they had a glamorous home tie against Manchester United. A crowd of 1,614 turned up that night, but the visitors won 3–0 thanks to a vintage display by a left winger by the name of Ryan Wilson. It was quite obvious he was going to be a superstar so what happened to him? Well, a few months later he changed his name to Ryan Giggs.

A LONG WALK

When Vale gained promotion from the Fourth Division in 1986 two fans made the bold statement that they would walk to the club's first away game the following season for charity. It could have been Chester, Walsall or Notts County, but the opening day fixtures pitted the club away to Middlesbrough! The two fans, Howard Dexter and Paul Foster, stuck to their task though and managed it in eight days.

That wasn't the end of the drama. Middlesbrough were in grave financial difficulties in those days and the day before the game were locked out of their Ayresome Park home! A postponement would have rendered the walk totally irrelevant but the game was hastily rearranged to be played at Hartlepool on the Saturday night. It meant a bit further to walk for the intrepid pair, but at least they had a game to go to. A good one as well, as Vale came from 2–0 down to draw 2–2.

It wasn't the first time fans had walked to an away game. In March 1973 a group of fans walked to a game at Shrewsbury Town to raise funds for the football club's Buy a Player fund. It raised over £500, a not inconsiderable sum in those days. The game was memorable as well, Vale coming from 2–0 down to win 3-2.

MOST APPEARANCES

In all competitions these are the top ten Port Vale players in the list:

Roy Sproson	836
Phil Sproson	500
Harry Poole	494
Ray Walker	440

Andy Porter	438
Dean Glover	430
Neil Aspin	410
Russell Bromage	402
Terry Miles	401
Basil Hayward	372

MOST GOALS

The all-important top ten in the list of leading goalscorers for the Vale in all competitions is as follows:

Wilf Kirkham	164
Martin Foyle	108
Stan Steele	95
Tom Nolan	93
Robbie Earle	90
Tony Naylor	89
Darren Beckford	81
Harry Poole	79
Adrian Capes	69
Tom Page	65

FRACTURED NOSE

John Poole's final game for the Vale was an eventful one. It was away at Mansfield Town in April 1960 and he was taken to hospital with a fractured nose during a 6–3 defeat. In those days there were no mobile phones and communication was a lot slower; so much so that John's wife Pat hadn't got a clue as to why he was so late after a game a reasonably short distance away. The phone eventually rang at 1 a.m. and it was the Vale manager Norman Low on the other end.

'Hello, Mrs Poole, Norman Low here. John's in hospital with a broken nose. The good news is he hasn't fractured his skull. Goodnight!'

I don't suppose Victoria Beckham had to wait that long when David did his Achilles.

GIANT-KILLERS' CUP

For a spell in the late 1950s to the early 1960s, the *Sunday Pictorial*, nowadays called the *Sunday Mirror*, awarded a cup every year to the club that had achieved the greatest giant-killing in the FA Cup. Port Vale were the recipients during the 1961/62 season. To earn it they defeated Second Division Sunderland 3–1 in the fourth round, after earning a draw at Roker Park. Over 28,000 rain-soaked fans witnessed the occasion and to commemorate the achievement the club received a huge cup, with the players being presented with a pair of gold cufflinks each. Obviously no expense spared in those days.

ROBBIE WILLIAMS GETS THE WINNER

Port Vale's most famous fan is of course the singer Robbie Williams and he would be delighted to score the winning goal for the Vale in a competitive match. Well in November 1994 he did – or at least his namesake did. Vale were playing a League One game at Barnsley and went a goal down. Billy Paynter equalised though, and 5 minutes later a cross by Jeff Smith saw Barnsley midfielder Robbie Williams knock the ball into his own net for the winner. A headline writer's dream if ever there was one.

FIRST GOAL

Port Vale's first Football League game took place in September 1892 when they were actually known as Burslem Port Vale. It was the opening day of the season for the newly formed Second Division and the Vale were away to Small Heath, nowadays known as Birmingham City. It started badly as leading striker Billy Beats missed the train and so they had to take the field with only ten men! It proved to be too much and Vale lost 5–1 to the eventual champions.

Wallace Bliss went down in Vale history, though, being their first league goalscorer. He went on to score two more in another 13 appearances, but he was released at the end of the season. Reports of the early games played by the club are very sketchy so it is difficult to pin down the scorer of the very first goal at any level, but it is purported to have been Jack Hood.

CORONATION CUP

To commemorate the crowning of Queen Elizabeth II in May 1953, a series of football games were played to raise money for charity. In the Vale's case they played local rivals Stoke City at the Victoria Ground on 4 May that year. Vale lost 2–0, but the crowd of 9,981 raised over £1,053 which was split between the King George VI Memorial Fund, the National Playing Fields Association and the Central Council of Physical Recreation.

NEIGHBOURS

Port Vale's local rivals are Stoke City, who have never been based more than 5 miles away. They have actually met almost 200 times altogether, but only 52 of those are competitive games. By that I mean national competitions, not things like the Staffs Senior Cup or the Wedgwood Trophy, etc. They have usually been tight affairs as evidenced by the complete record shown below. So tight in fact that neither side has managed to score 3 goals in any of the last 17 league meetings, which have only produced 30 goals in total.

Complete record:

	P	W	D	L	F	A
Home	24	7	9	8	27	28
Away	28	9	8	11	22	26
Total	52	16	17	19	49	54

Vale's biggest win is 3–0, which they have achieved on three occasions – twice in the 1925/26 season and at home in February 1932. Their biggest defeat is 0–4 in September 1931.

THE LEAGUE CUP

So often the bane of a Vale fan's life, Port Vale were often touted as having the worst record of all in this competition but it has changed a bit in recent years. In the early years first-round exits were commonplace and it took them 31 years to reach the third round – and that was after having a first round bye!

That first appearance in the third round was in October 1991 and 8,000 Vale fans travelled to Liverpool for the game. Expected to be summarily despatched from the competition, they produced a sterling performance to come away with a 2–2 draw thanks to goals from Robin Van Der Laan and Martin Foyle. Foyle scored again in the replay at Vale Park but Liverpool turned on the style a bit to win 4–1. A great occasion, though, in front of a crowd of 18,725.

The club reached the third round again in the 1996/97 season after defeating Crewe Alexandra and Carlisle United. This time their opponents were Oxford United and after a 0–0 draw at Vale Park, they succumbed 2–0 in the replay.

The best run of the lot came in the 2006/07 season when they reached the fourth round. Three Championship sides perished at Vale Park that season – Preston North End (2–1), QPR (3–2) and then Norwich City on penalties after a 0–0 draw – which precipitated a tie at Tottenham Hotspur in round four.

2,900 Vale fans travelled down to North London for the tie, and the club put up a tremendous performance in front of a crowd of 34,560. Leon Constantine gave Vale the lead, but Spurs took it to extra time before winning 3–1.

Further proof of Vale's resurgence in the competition came in the 2009/10 season. In the first round they defeated a team two divisions above them for the first time in winning 2–1 at Sheffield United and then beat their neighbours Sheffield Wednesday 2–0 at Vale Park. Unfortunately the draw gave them an away tie at Scunthorpe United and although taking it to extra time, they eventually lost 2–0.

Tranmere Rovers are certainly the team Vale least like drawing in the competition. They have played five times at Vale Park and have won the lot!

Mick Cullerton has the distinction of being the only Vale player to score a hat-trick in the competition, and he has done it twice. Once was in a 3–0 win over Chester in 1967/68, and then he did it again eight years later against Hereford United. That was a 4–2 win and Vale managed to lose the tie after being 4–0 ahead! They lost the return 2–0 and then a third match at neutral Shrewsbury 1–0.

Vale's biggest win in the competition is 5–1, which they have achieved on two occasions, both strangely away from home. The first was the second leg of a first-round tie at Wrexham in September 1983, and having won the first leg 3–1 they completed another club record, winning 8–2 on aggregate.

The other occasion was in September 1996 at near neighbours Crewe Alexandra, again after a first leg victory, which was 1–0.

The man who has made the most appearances in the competition is Phil Sproson with a total of 30, while both Mick Cullerton and Martin Foyle top the goalscoring charts with seven apiece.

Complete record:

	P	W	D	L	F	A
Home	53	19	10	24	72	80
Away	52	9	11	32	50	88
Neutral	2	0	0	2	1	3
Total	107	28	21	58	123	171

INTERNATIONAL VENUE

Vale Park has staged international football on three occasions so far, all of them at under-18 level. The first time was in November 1992 when Switzerland were the visitors for a friendly match. England won 7–2 largely thanks to a hat-trick by Robbie Fowler, two from Lee Sharpe, and one each from Kevin Gallen and George Ndah. David Beckham also played and the crowd numbered 2,541.

The second occasion was in September 1993 when Romania were the visitors for a qualifying tie for the European Youth championships. David Faulkner scored England's goal in a 1–1 draw watched by 1,204 spectators.

The last time was for a friendly against Norway in June 2005. Unfortunately the 5,000-plus crowd were only treated to a goalless draw.

PENALTY SHOOTOUTS

So far Port Vale have been involved in ten penalty shootouts, winning four and losing six. They have only met one team twice, Scunthorpe United, and they have beaten them both times, both away from home. Undoubtedly the most high-profile penalty drama was against Arsenal in the FA Cup third-round replay at Vale Park in January 1998. After a 0–0 draw at Highbury and a 1–1 stalemate at Vale Park after extra time, it all came down to the old twelve-yard lottery. Vale actually went in front, but Arsenal eventually triumphed 4–3 as Allen Tankard's effort blazed over. Arsenal went on to do the double that season.

The most penalties involving the Vale was 14 which has actually happened twice. First it was against Chesterfield in November 2002 and then the game at Bradford City in November 2009 in the quarter-finals of the Johnstone's Paint Trophy when both sides took seven each before a winner could be determined.

The only Vale goalkeeper to take a spot kick in a shootout was Mark Goodlad, and he scored against Chesterfield in November 2002.

The full list is as follows:

November 1986
v Scunthorpe U (A) Freight Rover Trophy   Won 4–3
February 1987
v Gillingham (H) Freight Rover Trophy   Lost 4–5

January 1998
    v Arsenal (H) FA Cup 3rd round   Lost 3–4
November 2002
    v Chesterfield (H) LDV Vans Trophy   Won 4–3
August 2003
    v Nottm Forest (H) Carling Cup 1st round Lost 2–3
October 2006
    v Norwich City (H) Carling Cup 3rd round Won 3–2
October 2006
    v Scunthorpe (A) Johnstone's Paint Trophy Won 5–3
      2nd round
August 2007
    v Wrexham (H) Carling Cup 1st round   Lost 3–5
October 2007
    v Morecambe (A) Johnstone's Paint Trophy Lost 2–4
      2nd round
November 2009
    v Bradford City (A) Johnstone's Paint Trophy Lost 4–5
      quarter-final

LEFT FOR A BIGGER CLUB?

When Phil Sproson left the Vale for Birmingham City in the summer of 1989 for a fee of £50,000, people could have been forgiven for thinking that he was joining a bigger club. Actually, Vale were in the Second Division while Birmingham were in the Third. To add to that, Vale's average attendance was 6,731 while Birmingham's was just 6,269, so just who was the bigger club at the time?

GREATEST EMBARRASSMENT

Since the Football Pyramid was formed, with various non-leagues being ranked in order, it has been possible to work out the number of places between clubs that met in the FA Cup. Prior to that, league clubs who lost to a non-league outfit were just deemed as 'having been beaten by a non-league club'.

Unfortunately for Port Vale the new format means that they have been on the wrong end of the biggest giant-killing of all time. 108 places separated League One Port Vale and British Gas Midland Division Chasetown when they met in the second round of the FA Cup in December 2007. The teams met at Vale Park first and when Luke Rodgers put the Vale in front it seemed that they were on their way to the third round. Mark Branch equalised with a free-kick from near the halfway line that eluded everybody, though, and it was back to Chasetown for the replay.

After a goalless first half, Vale were awarded a penalty in the 47th minute but Luke Rodgers blazed it against the bar. Just 8 minutes later they had another chance from the spot when Rodgers himself was brought down in the box. Rodgers took it again but the goalkeeper went down to his right to save. Vale dominated, but in the last minute Kyle Perry raced down the left and put over a superb cross for Danny Smith to head home the winner. It had all gone wrong for the Vale but that is how it is in club football. No other team has ever been beaten by a team 108 places below them in the pyramid.

Vale reacted by signing two of the Chasetown players in Kyle Perry and Chris Slater but it proved to be a step too far and both had departed within 18 months.

SUBSTITUTES

Substitutes have become an increasing influence in league football since first being introduced in 1965. First it was one, then two, then three, then five and currently seven, of which three can come onto the field.

Port Vale's first selected substitute was Clinton Boulton for a home game against Colchester United in August 1965. The first one to actually come onto the field was Terry Miles, who replaced Terry Lowe a couple of weeks later in a 2–0 victory over Stockport County.

The first Vale player to score after coming on from the bench was John Rowland, who joined the fray in time to score the winner against Rochdale (2–1), in January 1966.

The player who has made the most appearances from the bench is Martin Foyle, who came on a total of 81 times during his playing career at the club, between 1991 and 2000. Martin also holds the record of substitute appearances in a season, coming on 24 times in the 1997/98 campaign.

AMERICAN FOOTBALL

The grid iron game has been staged at Vale Park on a few occasions during an experiment in the late 1980s. The local American Football team, the Stoke Spitfires, arranged an exhibition game against Locomotive Derby in November 1986. A crowd of 1,627 turned up to watch in poor weather, and Vale themselves made enough money to offer the ground to the Spitfires for all their home games the next season, which was the summer of 1987. Crowds never really took off though, and it was the Spitfires who ended the arrangement as they struggled to keep going, eventually folding in 1992.

LONG-SERVING STALWART

Who has had the longest career with Port Vale? Anyone who knows a bit about the club will immediately answer Roy Sproson, who made 836 senior appearances and also managed the club. A good answer but wrong – his 28 years at the club were very commendable but Tom Holford devoted 36 years of his life to the Vale.

Born in Hanley in 1878, 'Dirty Tommy' as he was affectionately known in his playing days, played for Stoke and Manchester City, also winning one England cap before becoming Vale's player–manager in May 1914. In those days the Vale were a non–league outfit competing in the Central League.

His spell as manager came to an end in 1917 when he was conscripted into the army, despite being aged 39, but after the war ended he reverted to just being a player. He was part of the side that returned to the Football League in 1919 after Leeds City had been kicked out for making illegal payments.

He was making fewer and fewer appearances as age took its toll and he retired from playing in 1923, having played in every position for the Vale apart from goalkeeper. He then became the Vale's trainer, but in April 1924 an injury crisis meant that he was coaxed into playing a couple of games and he thus became the Vale's oldest ever player, at the age of 46 years and 68 days. At the time that made him the second oldest ever for any club, but even now he still ranks at number seven on the list.

This time he really did retire and went back to being the club trainer. In June 1932 he was appointed manager for a second time. The team finished 8th in Division Two under his charge in 1934, heights that they would never attain again for 63 years, but after five successive defeats that plunged them next to the bottom in October 1935, he was relieved of his duties.

He went back to being a scout, but also took over the post of trainer between 1939 and 1946 as staff were called up for the Second World War. Tom, a cousin of Vale's record goalscorer Wilf Kirkham, finally retired in 1950 at the age of 72, having spent exactly half of his life working for the club in some capacity. He died in Blurton, Stoke-on-Trent, in April 1964.

CHANGE OF NAME?

In February 1934 the directors of Port Vale decided that the name of the club was too parochial, it didn't reflect the name of the area and that most football fans didn't know where the team came from. Also it could be costing the club money in their opinion. Stoke Central and Stoke United were suggested and supporters were asked to vote on whether they wanted a change of name in principle. Surprisingly 3,737 voted yes with 3,633 against, also a high percentage of voters as the gate v Norwich was only 8,200!

This necessitated a shareholders' meeting in Hanley, and Stoke United was on the agenda. This wasn't too popular among the shareholders and they chose Hanley Port Vale instead, reflecting the area and keeping the old name. The Football League refused to sanction it part way through the season, but the directors forgot to raise it in time during the close season and the whole idea was abandoned!

The idea resurfaced four years later in 1938 as the club were really struggling for money. The names Stoke United or even Stoke North End were suggested once again. Surprisingly, judging by correspondence received from fans, no one appeared to object to this radical step! As time moved into July, there wasn't time to implement a name change before the new football season was due to start, and the suggestion was never raised again!

RECORD DEFEAT

Port Vale are the only club ever to concede double figures in a home league game. The fateful day happened in their first ever season in the Football League back in December 1892, when Sheffield United were the visitors for a Second Division game. In those days home games were played at the Athletic Ground in Cobridge. Snow had fallen heavily in the days beforehand and there were four inches of snow on the pitch at kick off. Regular goalkeeper Joe Frail, a gypsy, had reported in sick, but in truth he had probably foretold what was going to happen.

It was too late for Vale to get another keeper so the reserve half-back, Billy Delves, was pressed into action. Sheffield United had won their previous home game 8–3 and were 4th in the table while 8th-placed Vale had lost their previous three home games. The omens were not good. A snowstorm made conditions unbearable during the first half and keeper Delves did not enjoy his new role. At one point he lost his glasses in the snow as United rattled in five goals before the break.

At half time captain Fred Farrington took over between the posts but it made no difference as United scored another five for the game to go down in history. The crowd was only estimated in those days, and appeared to number around 500, probably owing to the weather.

It is not the only time the Vale have conceded ten goals in a game; they also lost 10–0 at Notts County in February 1895. At kick off they did only have eight players though, two had misread the rail timetable and one failed to turn up! Three substitutes were hastily pressed into action midway through the first half but in the end it made little difference. At least that game was away from home.

CLOUGHIE'S MATE

Peter Taylor will forever be linked with Brian Clough from their legendary days together in charge of team affairs at Derby County and Nottingham Forest. Probably less well known is that Peter was a goalkeeper who played in the Football League for Port Vale. He joined the Vale for a fee of £750 from Middlesbrough in June 1961, the club at which he first met Brian Clough.

He was only used as a reserve to Ken Hancock, but made his league debut at Bradford Park Avenue in February 1962. Ironically he played because Hancock had been injured in the previous game, against Clough's Sunderland.

Vale lost that game 2–1 with Roy Sproson scoring, and Peter returned to the reserves with Hancock fit again. At the end of that season he moved on to Burton Albion where he took the first rung on a successful managerial career.

SUNDAY FOOTBALL

The vogue for Sunday football first kicked off in the 1970s as an experiment to increase attendances. The Vale's first sojourn down that route occurred in February 1974 for a home game against the Third Division leaders Bristol Rovers. In those days it was illegal to charge admission for Sunday games, so clubs used to sell team sheets for the price of normal admission. On this occasion a team sheet cost 45p and production of that allowed spectators in the stadium, although by law the club had to have an open turnstile so that people could still get in without having bought a team sheet! It's fair to say that the club didn't publicise that scenario too much.

A season's best crowd of 8,505 saw Vale humble their lofty opponents 3–1 with 2 goals from Ray Williams and 1 from

Keith Leonard, on loan from Aston Villa. The Rovers reply came from none other than John Rudge, who went on to become the Vale's most successful manager.

The experiment fizzled out a few years later as attendances turned out to be no bigger than usual and police bills tended to be charged at double time, so nowadays the only Sunday fixtures are mainly for TV purposes or to avoid clashes with neighbours.

GOAL-LADEN CUP RUN

In the 1924/25 season, Port Vale only played in three FA Cup ties, but those games contained no less than 26 goals! Despite being in the Second Division, Vale had to begin their campaign in the qualifying rounds and the fifth such round gave them a home tie with non-league Boston United. Vale won 6–1 with three players scoring a brace each: Alf Strange, Wilf Kirkham and Billy Briscoe. For the sixth qualifying round they were pitched against another non-league side, Alfreton Town, this time away. The Vale won that one 8–2, despite a goalless first half-hour, the club's record away win. The same players scored their goals, only this time it was Briscoe (4), Kirkham (3) and one from Strange.

That gave the club a first-round proper tie at First Division Aston Villa. That is where it all went wrong, because despite being 1–0 ahead at half time, the Vale ended up losing 7–2! Wilf Kirkham was again on the mark with two goals.

AVERAGE ATTENDANCES

The highest average home attendance figure for league games for the Vale is 20,869 during the 1954/55 season, the club's first at Second Division level for 18 years. Attendances have only been accurately counted since 1920 (prior to that they were estimated), and the lowest home average was a mere 2,738 for the 1980/81 season. That season they finished 19th in Division Four, a year after their worst ever season when they finished 20th. The last time they averaged over five figures was in the 1963/64 campaign, and during the heady days of the 1990s, the best was the 9,174 they averaged in 1994/95.

MUNICH AIR DISASTER

An often recounted tragedy in the history of Manchester United, but how many people know that the death toll contained a former Port Vale player? Harold Donald Davies was his name, and at the time of the crash, he was a prominent journalist on the *Manchester Guardian*, the forerunner of the present day *Guardian*.

In his playing career he appeared 33 times in various competitions for Port Vale during the 1914/15 season when they were a non-league side, also scoring 5 goals. He originally pulled out of the fateful trip to Belgrade in February 1958, which crashed at Munich airport after a refuelling stop, killing 23 people. He was to have been replaced by John Arlott, but a last-minute change of plan led to Arlott staying at home, and he went on to become an esteemed cricket commentator. 'Donny' was 65 at the time of his death.

CONSECUTIVE APPEARANCES

The man who holds the record for the most consecutive appearances in a Vale shirt is central defender John Nicholson, who rattled up a total of 208 between 1961 and 1965. He was signed for £2,000 from Liverpool in August 1961 and did well enough to hold down a regular place. So well in fact that he became the first name on the team sheet, and he helped the side reach the fifth round of the FA Cup in 1962 and the fourth round two years later, when they ran his old club Liverpool very close.

After being left out in September 1965 for a game at Darlington when Terry Alcock was moved to centre-half, he immediately asked for a transfer. Despite protests from the fans, the directors granted it, and he was sold to Doncaster Rovers for £5,000. A year later he was tragically killed in a car accident, a day after his 30th birthday.

NEVER ON A SUNDAY

Since the 1990s, Port Vale have sometimes had to move home games from their traditional Saturday afternoon either because of TV obligations or to avoid a clash with neighbours Stoke City. It's proved to be a bad idea, because they have not managed a victory in the last fourteen such games stretching back to January 1995 when Tranmere Rovers were beaten 2–0 in a game covered by Granada TV. This is the full list since that game, which does not include Christmas Sunday games when full programmes can often fall on that day.

January 1995	v Tranmere Rovers	2–0
May 1995	v Notts County	1–1
October 1995	v Crystal Palace	1–2

October 1995	v Birmingham City	1–2
September 1996	v Bradford City	1–1
October 1996	v Stoke City	1–1
January 1997	v QPR	4–4
January 1998	v Stoke City	0–0
January 1999	v Liverpool	0–3
May 2000	v Wolves	0–1
September 2000	v Stoke City	1–1
October 2001	v Stoke City	1–1
December 2003	v Scarborough	0–1
October 2006	v Rotherham United	1–3
December 2007	v Chasetown	1–1

It's not so bad away from home, as Vale have defeated Stoke City (twice), Birmingham City, Barnsley, Huddersfield Town and Chester City besides winning the LDV Vans Trophy at the Millennium Stadium v Brentford during the same period.

DIRECT FREE KICK

Everybody interested in football has seen goals being scored direct from free kicks, and in recent years Cristiano Ronaldo and David Beckham have been at the forefront of them. Well it's a little known fact the first player to do score direct from a free kick was indeed a Port Vale player.

Up until 1903 it was against the law to score direct from a free kick, but upon the rule change it was the Vale who benefited first on the opening day of the 1903/04 season. Arthur Rowley was the man who went down in history blasting home the Vale's first goal in a 3–2 home defeat by Bolton Wanderers. Little did the 3,000 who were there that day realise what a piece of history they witnessed that afternoon.

COLOURS

Although presently known for being black and white, Port Vale have worn a variety of different colours during their long history. In fact they have been all the colours of the rainbow!

The first reported reference to the club's colours was in 1883 when they played in an all black strip. By the time they joined the Football League nine years later it had changed to red shirts and grey shorts. A brief flirtation with black and amber stripes with black shorts followed before in 1898 they wore red and white striped shirts and blue shorts! Obviously those shirts are associated with rivals Stoke City nowadays, but they weren't wearing them then!

In the early 1900s Vale went through a claret and blue phase, wearing stripes with white shorts, and then in 1913 it became a claret shirt with a blue 'V', again with white shorts.

After getting back in the Football League in 1919 they adopted an outfit of white shirts and black shorts for the first time, but it was changed in 1923 to red shirts and white shorts. This lasted until the appointment of Warney Cresswell as manager in 1936, who preferred to switch to white shirts and black shorts, which had been the change strip for a number of years. This encompassed the run to the semi-finals of the FA Cup in 1954, but for the debut season in the Fourth Division in 1958 they switched to black and amber striped shirts and black shorts. The feeling was that players look bigger (and presumably more menacing) in stripes!

They varied the stripes over the next five years, and even had amber shorts in 1961/62, but the reappointment of Freddie Steele as manager resulted in a switch back to white shirts and black shorts in 1963. Steele thought it was a more manly outfit! The club colours have been a variety of black and white ever since. They switched to all white in 1966, at the wish of general manager Sir Stanley Matthews, with it being popular due to the success of Real Madrid. Black shorts returned in 1972 and have stayed, apart from three all white seasons: 1976/77, 1999/2000 and 2007/08. The strip between 1974 and 1976 was an unusual one, as the white shirts had black and white striped sleeves.

Between 2008 and 2010 the club adopted black and white striped shirts with the black shorts, but ditched the stripes for the 2010/11 campaign.

ANGLO-ITALIAN CUP

The Anglo-Italian Cup was played between English and Italian league clubs. It first took place over four years between 1969 and 1973 before being discontinued, but it was revived in 1992. Port Vale entered it in the 1995/96 season. There was no qualification, basically it was the first eight teams in league table order from Division One, nowadays called the Championship, who wanted to enter.

In the group stages, Vale had to play four Italian teams, two at home and two away. It was the first time that the Vale had played a competitive game abroad, and their first game was away to Cesena. The club chartered an aircraft for the trip and apart from the team they filled it with a number of fans eager to see history made. They all flew home happy with a 2–2 draw under their belts.

Home games against Ancona (2–0) and Genoa (0–0) followed before the next trip abroad to Perugia. To say the Italian fans weren't too interested in the competition is a bit of an understatement as only 200 turned up for the game. This was a team which attracted 35,000 for league games!

The number of Vale fans there numbered 19, but it must be pointed out that over 50 were stranded on a coach in deep snow in the north of the country, and unfortunately missed the match. Those who were there saw a cracker, as Vale won

5–3 with Lee Mills scoring a hat-trick. The result was enough to put Vale through to the English semi-final (it was structured to feature an English club v an Italian one in the final) and they faced a tough trip to Ipswich Town where they had never won and only picked up one draw in thirteen previous visits.

The Vale had the bit between their teeth in this competition though and won 4–2, with another hat-trick, this time from Tony Naylor.

In the English final West Brom were beaten over two legs, and it was off to Wembley Stadium for the final in March 1996. Over 10,000 Vale fans made the trip, not surprisingly five times the number of Italians who made the journey in support of Genoa. Genoa produced a master class to go 5–0 ahead midway through the second half, but Vale fans had something to cheer when Martin Foyle scored twice to give the scoreline a bit of respectability. It may have finished 5–2 but the Vale had thoroughly enjoyed their first stint at European competition. Unfortunately it was to be their last, because the competition was then scrapped as a result of fixture congestion and apathy among the Italian supporters. The games in detail are as follows:

5 September 1995
Cesena (A) 2–2 (L. Glover, Mills)   Att. 820
11 October 1995
Ancona (H) 2–0 (Talbot, Guppy)   Att. 3,440
8 November 1995
Genoa (H) 0–0   Att. 3,282
13 December 1995
Perugia (A) 5–3 (Porter, McCarthy, Mills 3)   Att. 200
English semi-final
23 January 1996
Ipswich Town (A) 4–2 (Naylor 3, Foyle)   Att. 5,831
English final
24 February 1996
West Brom (A) 0–0   Att. 10,862

5 March 1996
West Brom (H) 3–1 (McCarthy, L. Glover, Foyle)   Att. 7,640
Final
17 March 1996
Genoa (Wembley) 2–5 (Foyle 2)   Att. 12,683

The final line up was:
Musselwhite, Hill, Stokes, (Walker), Bogie, Griffiths, Aspin, McCarthy, Porter, Foyle, L. Glover (Naylor), Guppy (Talbot)

BOAT RACE HAT-TRICKS

In the late 1980s Vale players managed to score a hat-trick on the same day as the University Boat race for three seasons running. The first one in March 1987 happened to be right next door! Barely had the race finished on the Thames when Vale went on to win 6–0 at Fulham, whose Craven Cottage ground borders the race route. On that day Andy Jones was the one to get a hat-trick as Vale romped to their record away win.

A year later Vale were at home to Doncaster Rovers as Oxford and Cambridge clashed oars and won 5–0 with Darren Beckford on the mark three times.

Remarkably it happened again in 1989 and it was Beckford who benefited for the second time. This time the victims were Notts County who were beaten 4–1 at Meadow Lane.

CONSECUTIVE SCORING

The man who holds the record for scoring in the most consecutive competitive games for Port Vale is Basil Hayward. A converted centre-half, Basil managed to score in 8 successive games in November/December 1953. Five of these were league games, plus three in the FA Cup, and he notched one in each game.

In purely league football the record is 7 successive games, a record held jointly by Hayward again, Wilf Kirkham and John Rowland. Wilf scored 10 goals in 7 games between February and April 1926, Basil Hayward managed 10 goals in 7 games in December 1952/January 1953 whereas John scored 8 goals in 7 games between September and October 1965.

GREATEST COMEBACKS FOR ...

Grimsby Town

Undoubtedly the greatest comeback from the dead that Port Vale have ever achieved was against Grimsby Town in December 1975. It was only a Third Division game between two teams in the bottom half of the table and only 2,789 spectators turned up, but they will never forget it.

It seemed they had made the wrong decision and should have gone Christmas shopping when Grimsby led 2–0 at half time. Just 8 minutes later they made it 3–0 and that seemed to be that. All of a sudden though, Vale came to life and scored a remarkable four goals in 10 minutes. Dave Harris headed home what seemed to be a consolation in the 59th minute, before Terry Lees scored 3 minutes later. Vale swarmed all over the Grimsby goal and Mick Cullerton equalised in the 66th minute before getting what proved to be the winner 3 minutes later! The crowd were just shell-shocked as were the Grimsby players, and there were still over 20 minutes to go, but there was no further scoring.

Huddersfield Town

When Port Vale visited Huddersfield Town for a first-round FA Cup tie in November 2008 they knew they were in for a hard time, not least because the Yorkshiremen were in a higher division. Although Vale took the lead through Louis Dodds, the home side were comfortably 3–1 ahead by the 79th minute.

Dave Howland then scored with an exquisite chip to make it 3–2 and suddenly Vale had hope. With 5 minutes remaining Dodds scored again and Vale fans celebrated as if they had got away with a replay. Not so. As the game entered stoppage time Vale were awarded a free kick on the edge of the box and Marc Richards curled it over the wall and into the net to make it 4–3!

Mansfield Town

A meaningless Third Division game in April 1987 at Vale Park. When Keith Cassells scored his second goal of the game in the 71st minute to put Mansfield 2–0 ahead, fans began to head for the exits. Vale's substitute winger Paul Smith had other ideas though, and he made three goals, in the 79th, 81st and 87th minutes to make the final score 3–2. The respective scorers were Darren Beckford, Andy Jones and Paul Maguire.

Southend United

A Third Division game played at Southend in September 1975. Vale looked dead and buried at half time when they were 3–0 down. In the second half though, goals from Gary Dulson, a Mick Cullerton penalty and Colin Tartt made the final score 3–3.

Rochdale

When Vale fell 3–0 behind at Rochdale in a Fourth Division game in November 1982, the local newspaper had to make a decision on their headline for that evening's sports edition, as communication wasn't as instant as it is nowadays. 'Heavy defeat for Port Vale' was the decision. That was the cue for Vale to make that look silly as they scored three times in the final 20 minutes, through Geoff Hunter, Ernie Moss and Jimmy Greenhoff to tie things up at 3–3 – a collector's edition of the paper if ever there was one.

GREATEST COMEBACKS AGAINST ...

QPR

Definitely a game to send shivers down the spine of any Vale fan who was there on that January 1997 afternoon, on live TV as well. It was a First Division (now Championship) game and Vale were good value for a 4–0 half-time lead thanks to goals from Dean Glover, Lee Mills, Jan Jansson and an own goal.

Five minutes after the break Tony Naylor had an effort kicked off the line that TV pictures proved was *over* the line, but little did anyone realise what a crucial moment that was. Debutant Jermaine Holwyn, signed from Ajax, headed into his own net midway through the second half but with 5 minutes left the game was seemingly petering out. All of a sudden Impey made it 4–2 and in the 88th minute Murray made it 4–3 to set the nerves jangling. I don't think anyone could believe it when Spencer made it 4–4 as stoppage time began! It was almost 13 years before any league club came back from 4–0 down, but no one will ever do it so dramatically.

Wigan Athletic

In April 1979 Wigan Athletic were enjoying their first ever season in the Football League and Vale visited their old Springfield Park ground on Good Friday. It did seem to be good for the Vale, as after an hour they were 3–0 ahead, the goals coming from Ken Todd (2) and Bernie Wright. After that it was not so good, from the Vale's point of view. Peter Houghton scored Wigan's first ever league hat-trick to level matters and then, even more galling, two former Vale players, Derek Brownbill and Mick Moore both scored to make it 5–3 for Wigan!

Sunderland

Port Vale were mid-table in October 1991 when they faced Sunderland in a Second Division game. At the time Vale had never beaten Sunderland in a league game but thought that run was about to be ended when they were 3–0 up after 56 minutes. Peter Swan, Martin Foyle and Robin Van Der Laan were on the mark for the Valiants, but Sunderland scored three times in just 11 minutes to level matters. Kieron Brady scored twice, with the other coming from Kevin Ball. Vale never recovered and finished bottom of the league.

Swindon Town

In March 2004 Port Vale were heading for the play-offs in League One and were in 7th place when they welcomed 4th-placed Swindon Town. All was going according to plan after an hour with Vale 3–0 ahead, thanks to goals by Billy Paynter, and Steve McPhee (2). Swindon clawed their way back into it though and made it 3–3 with 7 minutes to go, Parkin, Hewlett and Fallon doing the damage. The result had a profound effect on the end of season placings, as Swindon pipped Vale to the play-offs on goal difference!

THE CHAMPIONSHIPS

Port Vale have been Champions of a Football League division on three occasions.

1929/30 Third Division (North)

Vale won the championship at the first attempt following relegation from Division Two. It was a close run thing with Stockport County, as only one team were promoted in those days, and the title wasn't clinched until the penultimate game, a 2–0 victory at Doncaster Rovers. During this campaign the club achieved its best ever away record, of 13 wins, 5 draws and only 3 defeats.

1953/54 Third Division (North)

A record-breaking season if ever there was one, Vale romped to the championship only losing three matches on the way, also conceding a mere 21 goals, a Football League record that remained until 1997. Only 5 goals were conceded at home and the famous Iron Curtain defence kept thirty clean sheets, which is still a Football League record. Besides this, the team also reached the semi-finals of the FA Cup, becoming only the second Third Division side to do so.

1958/59 Division Four

This was the very first season of the newly created Division Four. Vale changed their strip to black and amber stripes, but struggled early on, as they didn't win any of their first five home games. After that though, they never looked back, and romped to the title, scoring a club record 110 league goals on the way.

ADMINISTRATION

Undoubtedly one of the darkest periods in Port Vale's history was when the club plunged into administration in December 2002. Probably the excesses of over-achieving during the 1990s, arguably the best ten years in the club's history when they had eight seasons in the Championship, had finally caught up with them. The club were around £2.4 million in debt, and owed around £600,000 to the Inland Revenue and so fell into the hands of Poppleton & Appleby to oversee the administration and try to sell the club on.

At the time there was no 10-point penalty, which at least avoided a serious relegation battle, but it was still a situation that threatened the club's very existence. Seven staff were immediately made redundant, including coach Mark Grew and chief scout Ray Williams. Buyers inquired, but the safest option for the future of the club was a bid by a group of supporters, under the banner of Valiant 2001.

A late bid which turned out to be from the Icelandic owners of Stoke City, unfortunately pushed up the price, but Valiant 2001 were confirmed as the preferred bidders by the creditors in March 2003. The full takeover, for around £1.6 million, was completed in May 2003.

UP, DOWN AND SIDEWAYS

After 97 seasons of League Football, Port Vale have achieved eight promotions and nine relegations. The promotions are as follows:

1929/30 to Division Two
1953/54 to Division Two
1958/59 to Division Three

1969/70 to Division Three
1982/83 to Division Three
1985/86 to Division Three
1988/89 to Division Two
1993/94 to Division Two

The relegations are as follows:

1928/29 to Division Three (North)
1935/36 to Division Three (North)
1956/57 to Division Three (South)
1964/65 to Division Four
1977/78 to Division Four
1983/84 to Division Four
1991/92 to Division Three
1999/2000 to League One
2007/08 to League Two

In 1957/58 Vale were sort of 'relegated' as that was the final season of Divisions Three North and South. The teams that finished in the top half of the two leagues went into the new Division Three, and those in the bottom half formed Division Four. Vale finished 15th and so 'went down again'.

Because of the club's geographical position in the centre of the country, they sometimes had to switch between the North and South sections of the old Third Division. These were the sideways moves:

1938 North to South
1952 South to North

LEADING LEAGUE SCORERS

Port Vale players have topped the divisional league goalscoring charts on four occasions, two of them joint.

1937/38	John Roberts	28	Division Three (North)
1967/68	Roy Chapman	25	Division Four (joint with Les Massie of Halifax)
1986/87	Andy Jones	29	Division Three
2003/04	Steve McPhee	25	League One (joint with Brighton's Leon Knight)

AUTOGLASS/LDV VANS TROPHY

The same competition, with two different sponsors, but either way Port Vale won them, the first at Wembley and the second at the Millennium Stadium in Cardiff.

1992/93

First round	bye	
Second round	12 Jan 1993	v Fulham (H) 4–3
Third round	2 February 1993	v Northampton Town (H) 4–2
Southern semi-final	3 March 1993	v Stoke City (A) 1–0
Southern final 1st leg	16 March 1993	v Exeter City (H) 2–1
Southern final 2nd leg	21 April 1993	v Exeter City (A) 1–1
Final	22 May 1993	v Stockport County (Wembley) 2–1

Bernie Slaven was the man who took the Vale to Wembley for the first time in their history with a vital equaliser at Exeter City.

Backed by over 25,000 fans, Vale played some great stuff in the first half, taking a 2–0 lead through Paul Kerr and Bernie Slaven. Stockport pulled one back through Kevin Francis but Vale held on to win 2–1.

The manager was John Rudge. Bobby Charlton presented the trophy to captain Dean Glover and the team lined up as follows:

Musselwhite, Aspin, Kent, Porter, Swan, Glover, Slaven, Van Der Laan (Billing), Foyle, Kerr, Taylor
Att. 35,881

2000/01

First round	9 January 2001	v Notts County (H) 3–0
Second round	30 January 2001	v Chester City (H) 2–0
Third round	6 February 2001	v Darlington (H) 4–0
Northern semi-final	5 March 2001	v Stoke City (A) 2–1
Northern final 1st leg	13 March 2001	v Lincoln City (A) 2–0
Northern final 2nd leg	20 March 2001	v Lincoln City (H) 0–0
Final	22 April 2001	v Brentford (Millennium Stadium) 2–1

Once again Vale defeated holders Stoke City on their way to victory, this time by virtue of the golden goal rule. Despite going a goal down after just 2 minutes of the final, Vale played superbly and eventually triumphed 2–1 with goals in the 77th and 84th minutes from Marc Bridge-Wilkinson (penalty) and Steve Brooker. The Vale manager was Brian Horton and the winning team was as follows:

Goodlad, Cummins, Walsh, Carragher, Burton, Smith, Brammer, Brisco, Bridge-Wilkinson, Brooker, Naylor
Att. 25,654

BERNI INNS

It is a little known fact that Port Vale played their part at the beginning of the Berni Inn Empire. In January 1954 the Vale won 2–0 at First Division Cardiff City in the fourth round of the FA Cup. It was a sizeable giant-killing and prompted a media frenzy. Possibly to make a good story, the Vale players put their achievement down to a pre-match steak dinner that they enjoyed in a restaurant called the Garrick in Hereford! Brothers Frank and Aldo Berni already owned a chain of cafés, but this gave them the idea of a chain of steakhouses! They backed up their convictions with action and opened their first steakhouse in Bristol a year later, soon becoming a worldwide hit.

BROTHERS

The brothers who have started the most games alongside each other are the Chamberlain brothers, Neville and Mark. They started 69 games together between 1979 and 1982. Older brother Neville was the club's first black player when he made his debut in 1978, and Mark came on to the scene in style a year later, becoming the youngest player to score a league goal for the Vale.

In the 1980/81 season they finished as joint top scorers in the league with 9 goals each, but surprisingly never scored in the same game! That changed in 1981/82 though as they notched in the same game on three occasions, the first being a 2–0 win at Crewe in October 1981.

Mark was becoming really highly rated and was tipped for the top as a succession of opposing left-backs were booked trying to stop him. In the summer of 1982, Vale had money troubles and needed to sell a player, and so Mark joined Stoke City along with goalkeeper Mark Harrison in a deal worth £180,000. An example of Mark's prowess was that within a month of leaving Fourth Division Vale he was in the England squad! He went on to win 8 caps, and nowadays is an academy coach at Southampton where his son is a first-team squad player. Neville also joined his brother at Stoke in a £40,000 deal in September 1982.

Two other sets of brothers have played together at competitive level, and one of them are the full-backs Bob and Peter Purcell, who managed 53 games alongside each other. Both born in Campbeltown, Scotland, Bob was the older brother and played for Queen's Park and Liverpool before joining the Vale in 1920. He made 68 appearances before being forced to retire from the game after suffering a broken leg in 1922.

Peter had played for Queen's Park and Rangers before joining Vale for a fee of £2,500 in 1919, a very large amount for the day. He made 166 appearances before being freed in 1924. After their playing days, the brothers ran a tobacconists shop in Hanley, Stoke-on-Trent, near to the Old Recreation Ground and retired in 1965 when both were in their seventies.

The other brothers to have played for the Vale together are the Kings, George and Ray, who clocked up eight appearances in the same side in 1949. George was a striker who scored twice on his debut but he only made ten appearances (5 goals) before being sold to Barrow for a four-figure fee in 1950. Ray was a goalkeeper, arguably the greatest the club have ever had, and he made 275 appearances, a record only beaten by Paul Musselwhite for a Vale goalkeeper, between 1949 and 1957.

This included the glorious 1953/54 season when Ray kept 29 clean sheets, an individual Football League record.

Other brothers to have played for the Vale rather strangely joined the club at different times.

Tom Page (1920–9) and Louis Page (1932–3)

Ray Hancock (1948–56) and Ken Hancock (1958–64)

Darren Beckford (1987–91) and Jason Beckford (1991)

FROM HERO TO ZERO

Ronnie Allen was a home-grown Port Vale player who aspired right to the top of the tree, but ended up breaking Vale hearts. Born in Stoke-on-Trent, Ronnie soon showed his prowess on the wing scoring 57 goals in a season for a team called Northwood Mission. Vale scout Eric Sweeney took him to Port Vale in December 1944, a month short of his 16th birthday and a year later he turned professional for a signing on fee of £10.

He soon aspired to the first team, becoming one of the youngest ever players, and scored a hat-trick against Aldershot aged just 18. Despite playing on the right wing, he was the club's top scorer with 13 goals in 1947/48, but his stature in the game brought about the inevitable transfer in February 1950.

First Division West Bromwich Albion offered £20,000 for his services, and being far higher than any Vale player had previously commanded, was instantly accepted. He went on to play for England and was the only player in the country to score goals in the first eighteen seasons after the war.

Vale had a superb season four years later and reached the semi-finals of the FA Cup in 1954. Their opponents were West Brom, for whom Ronnie was the centre forward. The heartbreak came later in the game, when, with the scores level, West Brom were awarded a penalty. Ronnie took it, 'the most difficult moment of my career,' he said afterwards, but scored to dash the hopes of his former team reaching Wembley.

CONSECUTIVE CLEAN SHEETS

The most consecutive clean sheets kept by the Port Vale defence is 7, a run they achieved between February and March 1922 when they were a Second Division outfit. They began the run at the bottom of the table, but had moved up to 18th when it finished. The games in question were as follows:

Notts County (H)	0–0
Hull City (H)	1–0
Crystal Palace (A)	0–0
Crystal Palace (H)	3–0
Rotherham County (A)	1–0
Rotherham County (H)	1–0
The Wednesday (H)	1–0

Welsh international goalkeeper Teddy Peers was the Vale custodian during that spell, and ironically he missed the game before and after that run, in which the team conceded goals!

On the other side of the coin the most consecutive games the Vale have failed to score in is five, all defeats in November/ December 1964. That was four league games and an FA Cup tie, and they have never gone five league games without a goal. They have completed four without scoring on no less than fourteen occasions, the last being in April 2009.

RE-ELECTION

Before the days of automatic relegation to non-league circles, teams had to go cap-in-hand to the league to be re-elected.

1892/93
Vale's first season in league football, and after finishing eleventh out of twelve teams in the Second Division, Vale had to seek re-election. It proved to be a formality, as the league was extended anyway.

1894/95
The Vale finished 15th out of 16, and so had to appear before the annual general meeting of the league. The bottom four had to endure this, and the voting went as follows; Lincoln 22, Burslem Port Vale 22, Crewe 18 and Loughborough 18. This meant that Vale were okay, but Loughborough replaced Walsall, who had finished above the Vale.

1895/96
This time Vale finished one place higher in 14th out of 16. Rotherham resigned, so it was just Vale and Crewe competing with eight non-league teams for three places. The voting went as follows: Blackpool 19, Walsall 16, Gainsborough Trinity 15, Burslem Port Vale 10, Luton Town 10, Crewe 4, Fairfield Athletic 3, Glossop North End 3, Macclesfield 2 and Tottenham Hotspur 2. So three non-league teams were elected and Vale faced two years in the Midland League.

1896/97

Vale applied for election to the league with three places up for grabs, but were unsuccessful, the voting being as follows: Lincoln City 21, Burton Swifts 15, Luton Town 13, Burslem Port Vale 11, Burton Wanderers 9, Nelson 7, Glossop North End 5, Fairfield 3, Crewe 2 and Millwall Athletic 1.

1897/98

Vale had beaten First Division Sheffield United in the FA Cup so were hopeful of being one of the three successful teams this time and their prayers were answered. The voting was: Lincoln City 21, Burslem Port Vale 18, Loughborough 16 and Darwen 15, with the unsuccessful applicants being New Brighton Tower, Nelson and Bristol City.

1904/05

A 16th-place finish out of 18 meant that Vale joined two others in applying for re-election. The voting was thus: Leeds City 25, Burslem Port Vale 21, Chelsea 20, Hull 18, Stockport 3, Clapton Orient 1. The next item on the agenda was to extend the league and when this was passed it meant that the first vote was totally irrelevant!

1967/68

The most unusual re-election plea the club ever had, as it had nothing to do with league position. In January 1968, an FA inquiry charged the Vale with breaking five league rules. They were:

- Several amateurs had been paid despite not being registered
- Associate schoolboys had played for the club which was against FA rules
- Extra bonuses were paid after a League Cup victory over Chester
- Illegal signing-on bonuses had been paid to players
- A director of the club had made gifts to young players

These misdemeanours had been minuted in club records so the greatest offence was probably ignorance. It was embarrassing for the manager, Sir Stanley Matthews, who had never even been booked during his career. A month later the club were fined £2,000, and then in March 1968 they were fined a further £2,000 and expelled from the league! This actually meant that the club had to seek re-election to the league at the end of the season despite finishing 18th in Division Four.

At the annual general meeting Vale were re-elected by virtue of 40 votes for and 9 against. Matthews left the club and his anger rose when Manchester United were fined £7,000 with no further action for similar offences! One rule for one....

FA YOUTH CUP

Port Vale have reached the quarter-finals of the FA Youth Cup on three occasions, 1966/67, 1977/78 and in 2007/08. The 1966/67 campaign involved a youth team put together by Sir Stanley Matthews so interest was a bit higher than usual – so much so that for the quarter-final tie at home to Scunthorpe United a crowd of 11,510 turned up! What made that even more remarkable was that it was nearly four times higher than the first team's average gate in the league that season.

Bolton, Wrexham, Shrewsbury and Coventry had been defeated during that run but unfortunately the Vale could only manage a 0–0 draw against Scunthorpe. The run ended with a 3–0 defeat in the replay, but nine of the Vale team went on to play league football.

In 1977/78 the team began its run from the first qualifying round and defeated Tamworth, Walsall, Leicester Beavers, Sheffield United, Blackburn Rovers and Hereford United to make the last four. Unfortunately they then came up against Crystal Palace, whose youth set-up was the envy of the football world at the time, and lost 3–0 at Selhurst Park. The Vale side included Neville Chamberlain, Russell Bromage and Phil Sproson who all went on to have long careers in the first team.

In 2007/08 the teams beaten during the run to the last eight were Nuneaton Borough, Doncaster Rovers, Swansea City, Bolton and Tottenham Hotspur. A crowd of over 3,600 saw the quarter-final home game against Chelsea, but their expensively assembled side proved to be too good and won 5–2.

THE BIG HOME WINS

24 September 1932
9–1 v Chesterfield Division 2 (Littlewood 6, Kirkham 2, Morton)
26 December 1958
8–0 v Gateshead Division 4 (Cunliffe 2, H. Poole 2, Steele 2, Jackson (pen), Barnett)
9 March 1929
8–1 v West Brom Division 2 (Pynegar 3, Jones 2, Mandley, Simms, Kirkham)
22 September 1930
8–2 v Bradford P.A. Division 2 (Jennings 4, Antiss 2, Griffiths, own goal)

28 September 1912

7–0 v New Brighton Amateurs FA Cup preliminary
(Gosnell 3, Dyke, Cannon, Walker, Stuart)

15 September 1947

7–0 v Watford Division 3 (South) (Allen 3, Hallam 2,
J. Smith 2)

10 April 1954

7–0 v Stockport County Division 3 (North) (Hayward 3,
Askey 2, Cunliffe, Tomkinson)

NB: Vale also beat Middlewich 16–0 in a friendly in 1884 and
Burton Rangers 14–1 in a Birmingham Cup tie in 1914.

THE BIG AWAY WINS

13 December 1924

8–2 v Alfreton Town FA Cup sixth qualifier (Briscoe 4,
Kirkham 3, Strange)

28 March 1987

6–0 v Fulham Division 3 (Jones 3, Smith, Walker, Maguire)

3 December 1927

6–1 v Blackpool Division 2 (Briscoe, Page, Antiss, Gillespie,
Kirkham, own goal)

9 September 1893

5–0 v Walsall Town Swifts Division 2 (Campbell 4, Beats)

3 December 1960

5–0 v Grimsby Town Division 3 (Portwood 2, Jackson, Fidler,
own goal)

13 March 2010

5–0 v Chesterfield League 2 (R. Taylor, Richards 3,
Davies (pen))

RAY KING

Arguably the greatest ever Port Vale goalkeeper and the statistics back it up; he holds the Football League record for the most clean sheets, 29 in 1953/54 (along with Gillingham's Jim Stannard in 1995/96) and is the closest that the Vale have ever had to having a current England player on their books. After that record-breaking 1953/54 season, Ray was chosen in a squad of forty that was to be trimmed down for the World Cup that year in Switzerland. As it happens Ray didn't quite make it, but did appear for England 'B'. In 1956 he was chosen for an England FA XI touring party that went to South Africa.

NB: although Vale kept 30 clean sheets in 1953/54, Ray missed one of them.

BASEBALL

Not something you'd really expect to find in a book about a football club, but a number of Vale players have actually been baseball internationals. Tom Page played twice for England in the 1920s, captaining them on one occasion, and his brother Louis played 8 times, being captain 5 times.

George Whitcombe also played baseball and captained Wales in a game against England played at the Old Recreation ground, Vale's home ground of course, in May 1930. Louis Page captained England that day, but didn't join the Vale until two years later or else Vale would have had both captains on their books. Harry Griffiths was another Vale player from around the same period who also played baseball for England.

SAME AGAIN PLEASE

Port Vale finished the 1979/80 season with a 3–0 home victory over Doncaster Rovers with goals from Steve Jones, a Neil Griffiths penalty and one from Russell Bromage. On the opening day of the following season, they were at home to Doncaster again and chalked up another 3–0 win, with two of the goalscorers being the same! Steve Jones was again on the mark, as was Neil Griffiths, who did take another penalty only to have it saved, but he headed home the rebound. Neville Chamberlain scored the third goal this time instead of Bromage though. Another notable fact about it all was that these were the only two goals that Steve Jones ever scored for the Vale!

WARTIME GUESTS

During the war years, players tended to guest for clubs all around the country, either close to where they were billeted or to raise morale among the locals. Port Vale had their fair share and they included Billy Meredith (Manchester Utd and Wales), Harry Betmead (England), Peter Doherty (Northern Ireland), Dennis Wilshaw (Stoke and England) and Frank Soo (Stoke and England).

SUPPORTERS' CLUB TROPHY

Probably to raise a bit of money from gate receipts, it was decided to introduce a new competition in the 1959/60 season, the Supporters' Club Trophy, to be played over two legs between Vale and Stoke. Both teams played their full line-ups (can you imagine that today?) and Stoke won the first leg 3–1 at the Victoria Ground in front of over 9,000. The return leg finished 2–2, so the trophy went south.

The following season Vale won the first leg 1–0 at home but lost the away leg 1–0. This necessitated a play-off decider to be played at Stoke, and Vale won 1–0 through an own goal. The competition was scrapped thereafter, being deemed more trouble than it was worth.

TEST MATCH

How many people knew that the Vale ground had once staged a Test match? No, they are not up there with Lords or the Oval, it was an 1890s version of the play-offs. At first there was no automatic promotion and relegation; the bottom three of Division One played the top three in Division Two in one-off games, with the winners taking a Division One place the following season. Thus at the end of the 1894/95 season, Stoke beat Newton Heath (later to become Manchester United) 3–0 at the Athletic Ground in Cobridge in a 'Test match'.

RESIGNATION

Despite finishing in 16th place (out of 20) in Division Two in the 1906/07 season, Burslem Port Vale had financial difficulties and were struggling to keep going. A loss on the season of £200 was unsustainable according to the directors and they appealed for investment. Unfortunately only one person came forward so they had no alternative but to resign from the league, just days after the annual general meeting. The Football League were angry as they had no idea of the club's difficulties but it proved to be a lucky break for Oldham who were elected in their place.

The club were actually wound up and were swallowed up by a club called Cobridge Church, who changed their name to Port Vale. Thankfully that kept the name going.

LOWEST GATES

Up until 1920 attendances were estimated, so since then these are the ten lowest league gates that the Vale have played in front of, and all are away from home.

982	Rochdale 30 March 1974 (1–1)
1,027	Aldershot 17 September 1985 (0–0)
1,052	Darlington 19 December 1986 (2–3)
1,144	Accrington Stanley 17 March 2009 (0–2)
1,215	Halifax Town 20 December 1980 (2–2)
1,227	Torquay United 5 November 1980 (0–4)
1,311	Northampton Town 17 April 1985 (0–1)
1,365	Doncaster Rovers 7 November 1987 (1–1)
1,372	Lincoln City 12 May 1984 (2–3)
1,389	Halifax Town 29 April 1986 (0–2)

As you can see, the Vale didn't win any of them! The lowest league gate they have played in front of at home since accurate records began was the 1,924 who witnessed a goalless draw with York City on 1 May 1982. In all competitions the lowest home and away gates are as follows:

994 v Hereford (H) 22 December 1986 (1–0) Freight Rover Trophy

569 v Newport County (A) 13 October 1987 (0–2) Freight Rover Trophy

NB: the attendance at the Anglo-Italian Cup tie away to Perugia in December 1995 was estimated to be 200, but no official figure was recorded.

ZENITH DATA SYSTEMS CUP

Probably the strangest named competition that the Vale have ever played in, it was the sponsor's name for the Full Members' Cup between 1989 and 1992 and the Vale competed in it for all three seasons. Full members were teams in the top two divisions, and Vale qualified by gaining promotion in 1989. They didn't do that well, never getting past the second round, but had notable victories away to Sunderland and at home to Blackburn Rovers.

PLAY-OFF NEAR-MISSES

Port Vale have twice failed to make the end of season play-offs on the final day of the campaign.

2003/04

Vale had flirted with promotion all season in Division Two (nowadays called League One) but only two wins out of eight in March left them in 7th place and doing the chasing. A last-minute winner in their final home game of the season against Tranmere Rovers meant that the play-off chase went down to the final day. The Vale's opponents were Rushden & Diamonds away, already relegated, and with one win from thirteen games.

The equation was simple; either a 7–0 win (probably a bit optimistic), or win and hope that either Swindon or Hartlepool lost their final game. The twist was that they were playing each other, and a draw would put both of them in the play-offs at the Vale's expense, 7-goal wins permitting.

Vale duly won 2–0 but the nightmare happened and Swindon did indeed draw with Hartlepool, so Vale missed out on goal difference. You couldn't get a bet on that match being drawn, the biggest surprise being that it wasn't 0–0! Swindon took an early lead but Hartlepool equalised 19 minutes from the end.

2009/10

Vale had spent the majority of the season in mid-table but were suddenly catapulted into the final play-off place (7th) in League Two with two games to go after defeating the champions elect Notts County 2–1. This meant that the team had matters in their own hands, but a trip to already-promoted Bournemouth ended in a disappointing 4–0 defeat, the club's heaviest of the season. They still had a chance on the final day though, and a crowd of 8,467, the club's best for six years and in terms of home fans an eleven-year high, turned up for the visit of Shrewsbury Town. To make it into the play-offs, Vale had to win and hope that two from Morecambe, Dagenham and Bury slipped up. Unfortunately Vale didn't win, drawing 1–1, but Morecambe and Dagenham won as well, meaning that the club finished 10th in the end, 4 points short of the promised land.

HE'S BEHIND YOU!

There was a pantomime moment in Port Vale's away game at Mansfield Town in February 1982. Vale were 1–0 down when an attack broke down and home goalkeeper Rod Arnold was ready to clear the ball down the field. He tossed the ball out of his hand but failed to spot Vale striker Mark Chamberlain lurking behind him. It was the end where the away fans were housed and so nobody made a noise as Chamberlain sneaked past the startled custodian and slid the ball into the empty net! Vale then went on to win with further goals by Ernie Moss and Tony Sealy.

BLOOD MONEY

When Port Vale signed a striker called Bob Blood in November 1919 for £50 from Leek Alexandra, fans wondered what was going on; the reason being he had served in the war, had a hole in his right leg, one leg was shorter than the other and his medical record suggested he should never play football again!

He soon put those theories into perspective by rattling in 26 goals to be the club's top scorer in the 1919/20 season. He carried on in the same vein in 1920/21 and one visiting goalkeeper broke his wrist saving one of Bob's penalties. He was far and away the leading scorer with 20 goals by February 1921 but then West Brom showed an interest in signing him. They offered £4,000, easily a record for both clubs, and one of the highest ever transfer fees at that time, so it was not surprising that Vale instantly accepted it. The fans were in uproar but the directors refused to comment. Later Bob revealed that he'd been told that if he didn't go, then the club would have gone to the wall!

PLAYER OF THE YEAR

The annual award for the Supporters' Player of the Year award began in 1967 and Roy Sproson was the first recipient. It then missed a year but has been in place from 1969 to the present day. It is voted for by the fans and just five players have won the award twice. The first to do so was Dave Harris (1974 and 1977) with the others being Ray Walker (1988 and 1991), Mark Grew (1989 and 1992), Neil Aspin (1990 and 1994) and Martin Foyle (1995 and 1999).

THE BIG HOME DEFEATS

10 December 1892	0–10 v Sheffield United, Division 2
12 December 1931	1–7 v Wolves, Division 2
2 February 1957	1–7 v Nottingham Forest, Division 2
5 September 1925	0–6 v Chelsea, Division 2
25 March 1957	0–6 v Sheffield United, Division 2
28 February 1987	1–6 v Blackpool, Division 3

THE BIG AWAY DEFEATS

26 February 1895	0–10 v Notts County, Division 2
23 November 1935	2–9 v Nottingham Forest, Divison 2
21 November 1931	3–9 v Spurs, Division 2
20 April 1935	0–8 v Brentford, Division 2
7 October 1893	1–8 v Ardwick, Division 2
8 April 1905	1–8 v Liverpool, Division 2

PFA AWARDS

Port Vale players have made the PFA divisional teams of the season on a number of occasions.

1981/82	Division 4	Mark Chamberlain
1982/83	Division 4	Phil Sproson, Russell Bromage, Geoff Hunter, Steve Fox
1984/85	Division 4	Russell Bromage
1985/86	Division 4	Phil Sproson
1987/88	Division 3	Ray Walker
1988/89	Division 3	Ray Walker
1992/93	Division 2	Ray Walker, Peter Swan, Ian Taylor
1993/94	Division 2	Neil Aspin, Dean Glover, Ian Taylor

EUROPEAN TROPHY

Port Vale have actually won a trophy on European soil. No, not the Champions League or the UEFA Cup, the TNT tournament played in Holland in 1992. It was a pre-season four-team tournament contested by the Vale, Go Ahead Eagles (Holland), De Graafschap (Holland) and Besiktas (Turkey).

Each team played two games and it was decided on a league basis, despite everyone not playing each other! Vale defeated De Graafschap 5–0 at Deventer and then lost 4–3 on penalties (after a 0–0 draw) against Go Ahead Eagles at Doetinchem. It meant that in the final game, Besiktas needed to defeat De Graafschap 5–0 to emerge on top, but in the event they lost 3–0, so the Vale won the tournament! Not many Vale fans saw Ray Walker lift the trophy, and it wasn't played for again so Vale kept the trophy for a number of years.

COMPLETE LEAGUE RECORD

In 97 seasons of league football, this is the Vale's complete record:

	P	W	D	L	F	A
Home	2,086	1,049	543	494	3,535	2,196
Away	2,086	428	525	1,133	2,089	3,768
Total	4,172	1,477	1,068	1,627	5,624	5,964

PLAY-OFFS

Port Vale have made the end of season play-offs on two occasions. The first time was in the 1988/89 season. The top three of Wolves, Sheffield United and the Vale were the best three sides in the Third Division that season but it was the Vale who were left to battle in the play-offs. Their fate was decided before the last day of the season, but on that last day Vale won and Sheffield United lost so they actually missed out on automatic promotion on goal difference. Because the play-offs were only in their third season, there was still the sense of disappointment that the team finishing third didn't get automatic promotion as they previously had done.

In Vale's case it meant playing-off with teams that had finished 9, 10 and 12 points behind them. In the first leg of the semi-finals Vale played away to Preston North End and despite going a goal down, drew 1–1 with Robbie Earle scoring. In the second leg Darren Beckford came to the fore with a hat-trick as Vale won 3–1. The play-offs were relatively new in those days, so there was no trip to Wembley on offer, just a two-legged final.

The opposition this time were Bristol Rovers with the away leg being played first. In those days Bristol Rovers played their home games at Bath City's Twerton Park stadium and tickets were soon snapped up by both clubs for a 9,042 sell-out. Just like the game at Preston, Vale were 1–0 down at half time but Robbie Earle equalised to give them the advantage. Away goals counted in those days as well, so a goalless draw would have sufficed in the second leg.

That important second leg, the Vale's most important fixture for more than 30 years, was played at Vale Park on 3 June 1989, the only time they have ever played a competitive match in June. A crowd of 17,353 witnessed a tense game in which Vale were on top but just couldn't make the breakthrough.

It was fitting though that in the 52nd minute a tried-and-tested method known as the 'MBE' produced the only goal of the game. A Simon Mills corner was flicked on by Darren Beckford and local boy Robbie Earle powered in the header to send Vale Park into ecstasy. The celebrations went on long into the night, as Vale returned to the second tier of English football for the first time in 32 years. What's more, it also meant a renewal of league games against local rivals Stoke City. The historic Vale line-up that afternoon was as follows:

Grew, Mills, West, Glover, Hughes, Jeffers, Walker, Earle, Porter (Finney), Futcher, Beckford

Vale made the play-offs for a second time in the 1992/93 season. Slightly different to 1988/89, four teams vied for the promotion places, as well as the Vale it was Bolton Wanderers, West Brom and Stoke City to add a bit of spice to proceedings. Vale had occupied the runners-up spot for three months from February until May but slipped up two games from the end by only drawing at Exeter City. On the same night Bolton were at home to Stoke, but unfortunately from a Vale point of view, their neighbours had already clinched the championship and lost 1–0 meaning that the Vale went into the last game of the season in third place. So, the Vale had to win at Blackpool and hope that Bolton slipped up at home to Preston. Vale duly won, coming from behind to win 4–2 but a second-half penalty won the game for Bolton to consign the Vale to the play-offs.

Their semi-final opponents were Stockport County, already in line to play the Vale at Wembley in the Autoglass Trophy final, which meant three games against each other in seven days. The first leg at Stockport ended 1–1 with Dean Glover on the mark, and in a tense second leg three days later, Vale won 1–0 thanks to a goal by Martin Foyle.

The third game of the trilogy against Stockport four days later was a never-to-be-forgotten day at Wembley when Vale triumphed 2–1 in the final of the Autoglass Trophy. 25,000 Vale fans travelled down that day, but in reality the play-off final a week later was more important. To play there twice in a week was just one game too far and the Vale following was reduced to around 10,000, against the 43,000 who followed West Brom there.

The game was a close one, but Peter Swan, the Vale central defender, was sent off and afterwards Vale capitulated to lose 3–0. At the time it meant that the Vale had achieved the highest points ever not to win promotion – 89. Sunderland have since taken that record with 90. Since that season the powers that be have moved the Autoglass Trophy in its various guises to an earlier date in the season so that no one will have to play two such high profile games in a week. The Vale line up was as follows:

Musselwhite, Aspin, Kent (Billing), Porter, Swan, Glover, Slaven, Van Der Laan (Cross), Foyle, Kerr, Taylor

The crowd of 53,471 was the second biggest the Vale have ever played in front of. The biggest was the FA Cup semi-final defeat – v West Brom!

PORT VALE – PREMIER LEAGUE?

It might sound a bit outlandish nowadays, but the Vale weren't that far off from lining up among the elite in 1997. In those days they were a decent Championship outfit but four wins in succession catapulted them into fifth place with just three games to go. What's more they were 4 points clear of 7th place, so a reasonable finish to the season would have meant a definite play-off place.

Vale's next game was away to Stoke City, a ground at which they hadn't conceded a goal in their four previous meetings, winning three of them. Unfortunately it went a bit wrong as Vale lost 2–0, but they still occupied 6th place, which became 7th a few days later as Crystal Palace won a midweek game.

Their next game was at home against Wolves, who had already qualified for the play-offs and were third in the table, but they proved too strong and went away with a 1–0 win. That left the Vale 8th and out of contention. On the final day they drew 1–1 at Crystal Palace, who eventually won the play-offs and had been 10th going into the final run-in.

In the end Vale finished 8th, their highest placing for 63 years, 4 points short of the play-offs. One point out of the last 9 needed to be 6 to have a chance at the end of season jamboree. I wonder how many years it will be before the Vale are that close again?

The Vale were also involved in a promotion chase to the top flight in the 1955/56 season, although there were no play-offs in those days, just the top two went up. With six games to go Vale lay 4th in the table, a point behind 2nd-placed Bristol Rovers. Draws in the next two games, at Stoke and Bristol City, left the league table looking the same, but then the wheels fell off. Three successive defeats v Nottingham Forest (0–2), Liverpool (1–4) and Leicester (2–3) put paid to their hopes. They eventually finished 12th, but the league table was so tight that they were only 3 points off 3rd place!

THE BIGGEST BOGEY GROUND
OF THE LOT

Throughout history, there will be some grounds that a team does well at and some not so well, but Villa Park takes the biscuit as far as Vale is concerned. It's just a string of defeats:

League games – 2–0 and 1–0
FA Cup games – 3–1, 3–0, 6–0 and 7–2
War League North – 4–0
Birmingham Cup – 4–0
Staffordshire Cup – 12–0
Friendly – 3–0
FA Youth Cup – 7–0, 6–0 and 1–0

Little wonder then that the club's FA Cup semi-final against West Brom, played there in 1954, ended in a 2–1 defeat!

THANKS – BUT NO THANKS

Dennis Booth was appointed as chief scout for Port Vale in the summer of 1999 – only to leave to take up a similar position at Nottingham Forest twelve days later.

Roger Jones signed for the Vale as a part-time goalkeeper, to cover in case of injuries, in July 1985. Ten days later he changed his mind and went elsewhere.

Craig Pead signed for the Vale from Brentford in the summer of 2008, but changed his mind the next day and stayed with the Londoners.

FLOODLIGHTS

The Vale's first official floodlights were opened in September 1958. They had cost £17,000, a not inconsiderable sum in those days, and were installed with the idea of being able to stage lucrative friendly matches to raise much-needed finance. The visitors were West Brom, who included former Vale player Ronnie Allen, and despite it pouring with rain, a crowd of 18,000 turned up to see the new venture. Vale won 5–3.

The first league game staged under the lights was a 4–1 win over Southport five days later, and the club went on to win the Fourth Division Championship that season. A new set was installed in October 1972, and John James scored in a 1–1 draw against Shrewsbury Town.

The Vale's first competitive game under lights marked the opening of neighbours Stoke City's lights in October 1956. Stan Smith scored the Vale goal in a 3–1 defeat. The team also played in Notts County's first floodlit venture in October 1962, drawing 1–1.

RECORD RECEIPTS

The most money taken at a Vale home game is the £170,349 banked for the FA Cup fourth-round replay v Everton in February 1996.

WILF KIRKHAM

Wilf holds the record for the most goals scored by a Port Vale player, a remarkable 164 in just 273 senior appearances. Just how good a record that seems is shown up by the fact that only one other player has ever topped the 100 mark, Martin Foyle with 108.

Local lad Wilf originally joined the Vale in 1920 but left to study at Sheffield Teacher Training College. A cousin of Vale stalwart Tom Holford, he returned in 1923 to turn professional and combine a teaching career alongside football, something he had always wanted to do. He made his debut in the 1923/24 season at Leeds and scored in his fifth game, a 3–1 win at Coventry City. He managed just the 7 that season, but really came to the fore in 1924/25, scoring 33 times in just 44 appearances.

That led to a call-up to play for the Football League against the Irish League and he scored twice in that as well. The goals kept coming, 35 in 42 games in 1925/26 including 5 in the two 3–0 defeats of Stoke City, and he set up a still-standing club record with 41 in 45 games in 1926/27, 38 of those goals in the league.

He dried up a bit by his own high standards but was still top scorer with 15 from 32 games in the relegation season of 1928/29. Vale were struggling for money at the time but the fans were not too pleased with the way they raised some. The board committed a cardinal sin in many fans' eyes by selling Wilf to rivals Stoke City for £2,800, the second highest figure they had ever received.

He did well down there, but after a broken leg he returned to the Vale in January 1932, as big a shock to the fans as when he left. His first game was a 3–0 victory over Stoke so any animosity was soon forgotten. He was back as leading scorer in 1932/33 with another 15 goals, but his teaching career was also doing well and he was appointed headmaster of Cobridge School. The authorities frowned upon him being a professional footballer as well as holding this prestigious post, so in a way he was forced to retire from the pro game at the age of 31. He then joined Kidderminster Harriers as a part-time player.

He also excelled at tennis and golf at county standard and later became a public house licensee as well. He died in Bournemouth in 1974, but will always have a place in Port Vale's history.

THE CHAIRMEN

Sam Bennion is the only man to both manage the club and be the chairman, although not at the same time. He also played for the club in a league game! Here is the full list of the club's chairmen.

1896–7	Edward Oliver
1897–1907	Robert Audley
1908–11	Sam Bennion
1911–13	J.H. Edwards
1913–21	Frank Huntbach
1921–6	Sampson Walker
1926–40	Frank Huntbach
1940–6	Tom Flint
1946–52	William Holdcroft
1952–8	Fred Burgess
1958–9	Jake Bloom
1959–60	Fred Burgess
1960–1	Jake Bloom
1961–3	Joe Machin
1963–5	Tom Talbot
1965–8	Fred Pinfold
1968–70	Arthur McPherson
1970–1	Mark Singer
1971–2	Graham Bourne
1972–7	Mark Singer
1977–80	Arthur McPherson

1980–2	Don Ratcliffe
1982–7	Jim Lloyd
1987–2003	Bill Bell
2003–present	Bill Bratt MBE

ALMOST A FULL HOUSE

During their 97 seasons of league football, Port Vale have met 118 different teams and beaten 117 of them. The one exception is Bootle, who they only met twice, in the 1892/93 season. The games both ended in draws, 0–0 and 1–1.

There are a few teams who have played league football but not come up against the Vale. They are Maidstone United, Aberdare Athletic, Ashington, Merthyr Tydfil, Stalybridge Celtic and Thames Association. Scarborough, Kidderminster Harriers and Boston United can also be added to that list, but while they have never met the Vale in league combat, they have played each other in the FA Cup.

NEUTRAL GROUNDS

The first time the Vale played a team on a neutral ground was in the fifth round of the FA Cup in February 1886, the first season the club had entered the competition. Vale had actually defeated Brentwood 2–1, but the visitors complained about the state of the Athletic Ground in Cobridge, which was very muddy. The FA upheld the appeal and another game took place at Derby County's ground. This ended 4–4 but Vale decided against travelling to Brentwood in Essex, as they couldn't afford it!

On New Year's Day in 1887 an FA Cup third round replay at home to Leek was abandoned before half time as the pitch was deemed too dangerous! Leek had protested about this before the kick off and another game was ordered to be played at a neutral venue. Stoke was the choice, but that was not possible as their ground was flooded.

The county cricket ground in Stoke was the next choice but Leek were so late in arriving that a lot of the Vale players had gone home. When they did show up the referee said the game was on and Vale were forced to field whoever they could lay their hands on. The weakened Vale side lost 3–1.

In December 1913 non-league Vale played Darlington of the North Eastern League in the fifth qualifying round of the FA Cup. A 2–2 draw at home was followed by the replay being abandoned in extra time when Vale were leading 2–1. The clubs failed to agree on a venue for the second replay, and so the FA ordered it to take place at Bramall Lane, home of Sheffield United. Vale won 1–0 in front of over 4,000.

The FA Cup semi-final between Port Vale and West Bromwich Albion took place at Villa Park in March 1954. Vale took the lead, but ultimately lost 2–1 to a penalty by their former player Ronnie Allen.

In the first round of the FA Cup in November 1969, Vale drew twice with then non-league Wigan Athletic. The venue for the second replay was Old Trafford, a big occasion for players and supporters alike. As it happens Vale won 1–0 with a goal in the last minute of extra time by leading scorer John James, who grew up as a Manchester United fan. The crowd was a very healthy 16,453. Isn't it a shame that penalties have taken these sort of occasions away?

August 1975, and Vale were paired with Hereford United in the first round of the League Cup. This was played over two legs, and Vale made the perfect start by going 4–0 up before half time in the home leg. Mick Cullerton scored a hat-trick. After the break Hereford pulled two goals back to lose 4–2 and then won the second leg 2–0 to tie things up. No away goals or penalties back then, so a third game had to be played.

It took place at Shrewsbury Town and Vale lost 1–0 to a late goal by former England international Terry Paine. So in effect, Vale were 4–0 ahead and lost!

The first round of the League Cup in August 1977 produced another all-square tie. Preston North End were the Vale's opponents and each club won their home game 2–1 and so another game was required. Stockport County's Edgeley Park was chosen as the venue and Vale lost 2–1.

Any neutral grounds the Vale have played on since then have all been at Wembley Stadium, and all have been dealt in further detail elsewhere in this book.

22 May 1993	v Stockport Co, Autoglass Trophy	Won 2–1
30 May 1993	v West Brom, play-off final	Lost 0–3
17 March 1996	v Genoa, Anglo–Italian Cup final	Lost 2–5

RESERVE CROWD RECORD

During the epic run to the FA Cup semi-finals that Port Vale enjoyed during the 1953/54 season, there were quite a few all-ticket games. The practice then was to sell these tickets inside the ground at reserve games. In those days the reserves played in the Cheshire League, with games being held on a Saturday afternoon when the first team were away. They normally attracted a few hundred spectators, but in this particular season they had crowds of 6,000 v Hyde United (tickets for the fifth round v Blackpool on sale), 7,000 v Winsford United (sixth round tickets v Leyton Orient) and a phenomenal 30,000 v Mossley in March 1954.

The latter was played a week before the semi-final when 25,000 tickets went on sale. This meant that Mossley attracted more fans than any league game that season, when the team won the Third Division (North) Championship! In actual fact only about 2,000 stayed to watch the game.

The first question it raises is what happened to the ticket requests of the loyal fans who followed the first team away from home when this was going on? Maybe they had special dispensation? It's the sort of sharp practice that some clubs probably wish they put into practice in the present day and age!

FANZINES

The fanzine explosion in the 1980s led to some Vale fans creating one in February 1989, and it hit the streets with the name *The Memoirs of Seth Bottomley*. It was named after a fictional character who supposedly watched the Vale 'in the good old days'. It was very popular for a number of years before folding and nowadays the club has two fanzines vying for custom. One is called *Derek I'm Gutted* after a quote by manager Brian Horton to a local reporter following a defeat at Tranmere, while the other is called *The Vale Park Beano*, Beano being a term used by the local newspaper referring to a councillor's junket at the Britannia Stadium, Stoke City's home ground.

ARRESTING DEBUT

When goalkeeper Walter Smith was signed by Port Vale in October 1920 he was in line to make his debut at South Shields a few days later. With it being a long distance to travel, the team stayed overnight at the Regent Hotel. On the morning of the game the police turned up at the hotel and arrested Walter on a charge of assaulting a chambermaid! He was released on bail but it's fair to say it must have affected his afternoon's work as Vale were thumped 6–1. The case went to court a few weeks later but Walter was acquitted.

SPEEDWAY

In the summer of 1969 Port Vale's total debt had risen to over £178,000, so action needed to be taken to reduce it. To raise funds on a regular basis the directors decided to introduce speedway at Vale Park, a sport that had proved very popular when staged 2 miles away in Hanley a few years before.

Valiant Speedway Enterprises were behind the venture and had been awarded a place in Division Two of the National Speedway League and were delighted when the council passed their plans. The local residents were not so delighted though, and soon mustered up a 2,000-signature document against the plans which they presented to their local MP and the council. Their main gripe was noise and also disruption.

In the face of this, and no doubt the thought of being voted out next time, the council reversed their decision and refused the application. Vale appealed and responded by producing 3,000 signatures in favour, no doubt the fans of the club, but there was no moving them again and it has never been mentioned since.

THEY DIED AT THEIR DESKS

Two of Port Vale's managers have unfortunately died while in office. Former England international Joe Schofield had been in charge for 10 years, a period only beaten by John Rudge, when he became seriously ill in September 1929. He died aged only 58.

In June 1951 Gordon Hodgson, who had been in charge for 5 years, had been battling cancer for a while and died. His funeral was conducted by one of his own players, the Revd Norman Hallam.

VALE PARK

Vale Park has been the club's home for 60 years. In 1943 the club president, Major Huntbach, died and so his debentures were all called in, leaving the football club in a dire financial situation. The upshot was that the directors had no option but to sell the Old Recreation Ground to the council for £13,500. This didn't go down at all well with both fans and shareholders but nothing else would have saved the club.

A rent was negotiated so that they could still play there for a few years after the war ended and the search was on for a new ground. They identified a site in Burslem that was an old marl hole, and mainly just used for waste-tipping. Money needed to be raised to turn it into a football ground, which became easier after the war ended and league football resumed, and various other methods were deployed to transform the 18-acre site. It took six years altogether and was originally a lavish project that was going to build 'The Wembley of the North' with a capacity of 70,000.

It cost £50,000 altogether but not enough finance was forthcoming to finish the project and it opened with a capacity of 40,000 which was virtually all open terrace. The first game in August 1950 was preceded by an opening ceremony that revealed that it was to be called Vale Park. Their opponents were Newport County for a Third Division (South) encounter and a crowd of 30,042 saw the Vale win 1–0 with Walter Aveyard going down in history as the man who scored the first goal on the ground.

Capacity increased to 50,000 by 1959 which was almost breached a year later for an FA Cup tie against Aston Villa, but the present all-seated capacity is around the 18,000 mark. It went all-seated by the early 1990s.

SNOW JOKE

When Port Vale played Hartlepool on a Monday night in March 1970, the pitch was snow covered, as were most of the surrounds. Half time was 0–0 and as the teams came out for the second half the Hartlepool goalkeeper Tony Bircumshaw ran towards the open Hamil Road end of the ground to take his place.

As he approached the net a huge hail of snowballs rained down upon him and he retreated to the halfway line! Every time he ventured towards the goal, more snowballs were thrown as indeed they were at the police who tried to restore calm. After a 5-minute delay, the storm relented but the keeper must have still been a bit nervous as Vale scored twice through Clinton Boulton within 3 minutes of the restart and went on to win 3–0.

THEY SAID IT ...

'Darren Beckford was a brilliant striker for the Vale, but a nightmare to manage. It was like throwing a blancmange at the wall, you just hope that a bit of it sticks!'

John Rudge

'When the coach, Reg Berks, invited me up to the Vale for a trial, he didn't realise that I was the nephew of his friend Roy Sproson, who happened to be the Vale manager at the time! There was never any nepotism though, Roy had been sacked before I turned professional.'

Phil Sproson

'I grew up as a Vale supporter, as being born and bred in Hanley, it was only a ten-minute walk to where their home ground was in those days. I always used to go to their home games when the gates opened about half an hour before the end right up until when I signed for Stoke City. It was ironic that my first goal for Stoke was scored against the Vale in Hanley.'

Sir Stanley Matthews

'I had six great years as a player at the Vale, some of the happiest times of my life and I didn't want to leave. After a 2–2 draw at Crystal Palace in 1976 though, the manager Roy Sproson came in and told me a fee of £30,000 had been agreed with Brighton and that their chairman was waiting to drive me down there to complete the move! My head was in a whirl and I didn't even have time to ring my wife, but that's how things were done in those days. It turned out to be a good move for me though, as I ended up playing in the First Division.'

Brian Horton

BEWARE THE TRENTHAM TERROR

Pre-season training under Micky Adams is never easy, but it took another twist for winger Lewis Haldane in the summer of 2010. He was running up the hills of Trentham, in Stoke-on-Trent, with the rest of the squad, when he was bitten by an insect. A hazard of the job you may think, but his ankle swelled up to twice the size and he was admitted to hospital, a stay that lasted for twelve days! During antibiotic treatment he lost over two and a half stone which meant that he missed the start of the 2010/11 season.

The good news when he came out was that he still had to do some pre-season training!

AND FINALLY ...
THE ONE THAT GOT AWAY

In the mid–1980s manager John Rudge was always scouting for new players and he came upon one he quite liked the look of at West Brom. Although not in their first team, the Baggies knew of the teenager's potential and wanted £50,000 for his services. Vale chairman Jim Lloyd almost had a coronary at the thought of spending such an amount, at the time £10,000 more than the club had ever spent for a player.

Put in a nutshell, the club simply couldn't afford him. His name? Steve Bull, who later broke all sorts of goalscoring records with Wolves following a £65,000 transfer. He thanked Vale for their interest by scoring 13 times in 17 appearances against them, including 6 in his first two matches!